JAMIE OLIVER'S FOOD ESCAPES

Also by Jamie Oliver

Jamie Oliver's
FOOD
ESCAPES

Over 100 Recipes from
the Great Food Regions
of the World

Photography by David Loftus
Design by Interstate Associates

HYPERION
NEW YORK

Published by arrangement with Michael Joseph / The Penguin Group

www.penguin.com
www.jamieoliver.com

ISBN: 978-1-4013-2441-4

Hyperion books are available for special promotions and premiums.
For details contact the HarperCollins Special Markets Department in
the New York office at 212-207-7528, fax 212-207-7222, or email
spsales@harpercollins.com.

First U.S. Edition

10 9 8 7 6 5 4 3 2 1

JamieOliver.com

To David "Lord" Loftus, my dear friend, and a world-renowned photographer.

We've worked together for twelve years, and hopefully we'll be shooting together until we're hobbling around on walkers! Thanks so much for your hard work, wonderful pictures and friendship. Love, Jamie

SPAIN ITALY SWEDEN MOROCCO GREECE FRANCE

If I've learned anything over the years, it's to follow my gut. After hopping on a cheap round-trip flight to Morocco and spending a few short but brilliant days tasting my way through the markets and alleyways of Marrakesh, my instincts were telling me I had to take more of these trips. All those new flavors, sights, sounds and smells were like a breath of fresh air to me, and I came home excited and full of new ideas ... which is where this book comes in.

That one trip gave me the push I needed to finally get round to seeing some of the other places I'd been hearing about for years. Athens and the Greek islands, Venice, the Midi-Pyrénées in France, sunny Andalucía in Spain and the absolutely beautiful city of Stockholm were top of my list and only a few hours from my home in the UK. Each trip was short, sweet and packed with mind-blowingly good food. *Jamie Oliver's Food Escapes* is my way of bringing the food on my doorstep to yours.

First and foremost, I hope the recipes in this book excite you and become a part of your life. I've collected my own versions of each country's star dishes: the flamboyant paella of Spain, exotic Moroccan tagines, zingy fresh Greek salad, lovely Swedish meatballs and some downright gorgeous French desserts. I've also included lots of lesser-known but equally incredible dishes – things I stumbled across in restaurants, tapas bars, back-alley street stalls and family homes. To me, they are proof that when you keep your eyes, and your mind, open you can unearth some real gems. If you've spent time in any of the countries I've covered here, chances are you'll come across recipes in these pages for things you may have eaten, and loved, on your own travels. If that's the case, I hope my recipes do the memories you have of that food justice, and help you to recreate them in your own kitchens.

Not only do I want this book to drag you out of any "What shall I have for dinner?" ruts, I want it to inject you with a bit of impulsiveness, because the whole point of this book is to show how easy, how valuable, how exciting, it can be to hop in your car or on a bus or plane and fill up on other cultures. The world is such a melting pot these days that you don't necessarily even need to leave your own country to do this. If you live near a cool city with pockets or neighborhoods full of exciting food you've never tried before, go there! I genuinely believe just a few days out of your comfort zone will give you optimism and positivity and get you ready to face the daily routine once you're back. So I also hope this becomes more than a cookbook to you: I hope it becomes a book that makes you want to jump up and visit new places too.

In Europe, there are now low-cost carriers that can get you to another country in less time, and for less money, than it costs to travel on the train to some British cities! So if you find yourself in Europe, it's well worth hunting down a bargain, whether it's from London to Madrid or Manchester to Paris, go for it! Every now and then, looking elsewhere for inspiration is a brilliant thing to do. In a funny way, it even helps you to appreciate all the things that are great about where you live.

Pick a destination, go there, be open-minded and talk to the locals. Eat the things they eat and go where they go. You don't need to speak the language, just as long as you've got a smile on your face – people will be jumping over themselves to show you the stuff they're proud of.

Often, the things they'll be most proud of won't be the fanciest dishes on the menu – they'll be the simple, hearty stews they feed their families, or the spicy meatballs they stuff inside flatbreads. I love that, because one of the things that gets me out of bed every day, and keeps me doing the things I do, is a deep personal belief that you don't have to have loads of money to feed yourself, or your family, like a king. I hate hearing people say otherwise because I know deep down it's not true. And from the simple country soups of France to the nourishing risottos of Venice, I was reassured once again that the simplest, most humble cooking is often the best.

So please, enjoy this book, have fun with these recipes, then go on your own short escapes. You can spend less money than you would if you were getting trashed for the weekend in your home town, and you'll have a head full of amazing memories. I've put together city guides for the places I went in this book. So if you're planning a trip, or want to let me in on some must-go places you've discovered, go to www.jamieoliver.com/cityguides.

I guess what I'm saying is, when you come across something great and beautiful, never ever keep it to yourself. Write it down, take a picture of it, then take it home and make sure your family, your kids and your friends hear about it. That's what makes the world go round. Enjoy it!

Love, Jamie

A note about buying fish and seafood: Always buy fish with standards in mind and remember that you get what you pay for. With wild fish, look for reassurance on the pack that it has been sustainably sourced without harming fish stocks. With farmed fish, look for reassurance that it has been farmed in a way that is humane for the fish and doesn't harm the environment.

¡BUEN APETITO! BUON APPETITO! Καλή όρεξη!
BON APPÉTIT! بالهنا و الشـفاء! SMAKLIG MÅLTID!

SPAIN

SPAIN

Spain is a country you can fall in love with right away. It has beautiful mountains and coastlines, exciting cities full of amazing architecture, warm, lovely people and great weather.

Ánd to top it all off it also has a perfect mixture of modern convenience and old-world charm. This definitely comes across in its food culture: artisan producers all over the country still use traditional methods to make their world-class cured hams, chorizo sausages, cheeses, oils and wines. Cutting-edge Spanish chefs like Ferran Adrià of the soon-to-close El Bulli (voted best restaurant in the world for the third year running) are pushing Spanish food to a whole new level. You only have to look at the northern town of San Sebastián, which has more Michelin-starred restaurants per capita than any other town in the world, to find proof that Spanish cooking is in a very good place.

Spain's location and history have given it a really rich collection of genius and exciting dishes. As a gateway from North Africa to the Mediterranean, Spain was where many ingredients that were making their way from one country to another stopped off and over time became incorporated in the cooking. The Greeks introduced olives and olive oil, and the Moors – Arabs from North Africa – who ruled Spain for 500 years really shaped the direction of modern Spanish food by bringing fantastic stuff like rice, fruits, nuts and spices such as saffron, nutmeg and cinnamon with them. Another big injection of ingredients came in the late 1400s from the newly discovered Americas. Suddenly, all sorts of wonderful things like tomatoes, beans, potatoes, chocolate and vanilla started turning up and the flavors went up another few notches!

The more I learned about the history of Spain on this trip, the more I started spotting those different influences all around me: in the incredible plates of paella, the kicks of herbs and spices in the cured sausages, the little cups of gazpacho, the candied fruits and pastries in the bakeries ... there are so many wonderful surprises in Spanish cooking.

If the number of Spanish restaurants and tapas bars I've seen around the world is anything to go by, Spanish food is on the up in popularity. So it is bizarre to see some tourists in Spain turning their noses up at the wonderful local grub and complaining that they can't get the same old boring food that they'd get back home. What a missed opportunity! The trick to discovering the "real" Spain is to jump in a car and keep driving until there's not a chain restaurant or fast-food joint in sight.

I decided to spend most of my trip finding out what the mountains of Andalucia had to offer. I headed north from Málaga to the beautiful old town of Ronda, birthplace of modern bullfighting and home to the Puente Nuevo, the jaw-dropping bridge that joins the mountains on either side of the El Tajo gorge. It's a spectacular place and turned out to be a great base for traveling around the smaller villages and towns of the area.

Like most of Spain, this part of Andalucia is blessed with plenty of sunshine, so although the land itself is quite rocky and steep, all the classic sunshine crops like olives, grapes and tomatoes grow in abundance. There don't seem to be quite as many big supermarkets as we're used to, but I put that down to the fact that a lot of people – even in towns – still grow their own onions and veg in whatever patch of land they have access to. There are also plenty of smaller suppliers to fill the gaps in the market, so the locals are never short of good food.

In this chapter I'm going to give you my versions of the Spanish dishes we've all heard of before, like paella and gazpacho, as well as lots of little ideas for tapas – which I'll talk more about later. The Spanish approach to food is simple, but powerful, and it's not about delicate fancy cooking. It's about taking really great ingredients like the freshest seafood, carefully cured ham and beautiful sun-ripened tomatoes and turning them into something delicious, using little hits of herbs and spices to keep things exciting and fun.

BEST CHORIZO AND TOMATO SALAD IN THE WORLD

Serves 4 as a light meal

- 1 raw chorizo sausage (approximately 8 ounces), roughly sliced
- olive oil
- 3 large ripe tomatoes, roughly chopped
- 3 handfuls (9½ ounces) of cherry tomatoes, quartered, smaller ones halved
- 3 scallions or 1 shallot, trimmed or peeled and finely sliced
- sea salt and freshly ground black pepper
- Spanish extra virgin olive oil
- sherry vinegar
- a small bunch of fresh flat-leaf parsley (you could also use basil or mint), leaves picked and finely chopped
- 2 cloves of garlic, peeled and finely sliced
- a rustic loaf of bread, to serve
- optional: goat's cheese, to serve
- optional: pata negra or Serrano ham, to serve

So many people live their lives eating the most boring tomato salads and there's no need to! Using really ripe sweet tomatoes and a hero ingredient like chorizo means you'll end up with something ridiculously good.

Chorizo is the king of sausages in Spain, and rightly so because it's so versatile: you can buy uncooked chorizo, which you can grill or fry, or precooked chorizo, which you can eat right away. The flavors range from mild to really spicy, so it's the perfect ingredient for flavoring all sorts of dishes. Also, if you haven't used sherry vinegar before, please do. It will transform your dressings.

Fry the sliced chorizo in a pan over medium heat with a lug of olive oil. Stir it with a wooden spoon occasionally while you prepare your tomatoes and scallions. Put them into a bowl with a good pinch of salt and pepper, a lug of extra virgin olive oil and a splash of sherry vinegar. Sprinkle over the chopped parsley, toss everything together, then put aside.

By now, your chorizo should be getting crispy, with lots of beautiful fat cooking out of it; this is where the magic happens. Add the sliced garlic to the pan and keep it moving around. You don't want it to burn, so as soon as it starts to smell fantastic, get the pan off the heat and pour in a small splash of sherry vinegar to stop it cooking further. Stir, then spoon the crispy chorizo and some of its lovely flavored oil and garlic over the salad (if you've got any leftover fat in the pan, pour it into a jam jar and store it in the fridge – if you rub it all over a chicken before roasting it will add the most incredible flavor).

Toss your salad and serve it right away. You'll definitely want some hunks of bread to mop up all that spicy garlicky dressing, and maybe some nuggets of good goat's cheese on the side. I also like to serve this with a few slices of pata negra – it's a wonderfully aromatic cured ham from Spain's famous Iberian pigs, and you should be able to find it in specialty grocery stores. You can also substitute Serrano ham, which might be easier to find.

MY MOORISH PORK CHOPS

Serves 4

For the chops
- a few sprigs of fresh oregano or marjoram, leaves picked
- sea salt and freshly ground black pepper
- a small handful of raisins
- good quality dry sherry
- Spanish extra virgin olive oil
- 4 large, thick pork chops (approximately 12 ounces each), bone-in, the best quality meat you can afford

For the beans
- trimmed fat from a few slices of pata negra, and some pata negra trimmings (or 2 slices bacon, roughly chopped, or pancetta)
- olive oil
- 1 red onion, peeled and finely chopped
- 1 large red pepper, deseeded and roughly chopped
- a few sprigs of fresh rosemary, leaves picked
- a few fresh bay leaves
- 1 x 19 ounce jar of white beans or butter beans, drained
- 14 ounces Swiss chard, stalks trimmed, or spinach leaves

When the Moors invaded Spain they brought grapes and dried fruits with them. Their love of mixing dried fruits with meats definitely left its mark on Spanish cooking and this is my nod to that time in Spain's history. Cut into these big tender chops and you'll get sweet juicy flavors inside perfectly cooked meat. Go to a good butcher and ask for chops that are an inch thick, ideally with two different colors of meat on them: the sweet darker meat, and the leaner eye meat. Then head to any good food store for the jarred beans. Spanish beans are like the Bentley of beans, so although they cost a bit more than the canned ones they make all the difference.

Pound most of your oregano leaves with a small pinch of salt and pepper in a pestle and mortar. Roughly chop the raisins, then add them to the pestle and mortar with a splash or two of sherry and a splash of extra virgin olive oil. Muddle everything together to make a paste, then put to one side for a minute.

Lay each pork chop in front of you so the side with the fat is farthest away. Carefully insert a knife into the side nearest you and move it around to make a pocket inside. Use your fingers to fill each pocket with the raisin paste. Look at the picture to see what I mean, or go to www.jamieoliver.com/how-to.

Fry the strips of fat from your pata negra or bacon in a medium pan over high heat for a few minutes, then add the trimmings (or bacon) and a drizzle of olive oil. Stir in the chopped onion and pepper, then turn the heat down and cook for about 5 more minutes, or until the vegetables have softened. Roughly chop your rosemary leaves and add those to the pan along with your bay leaves.

Add your beans to the pan with 1½ cups of water. Stir, then leave to simmer away for about 20 minutes. Keep an eye on the beans and add a splash more water if they look dry.

Get a grill or grill pan really hot. Rub some olive oil and a good pinch of salt and pepper all over the pork chops. Put them on the very hot side of your grill and sear them for 2 to 3 minutes on each side to get some good color going, then move them to the gentler side of the grill so they can cook slowly. If you're using a grill pan, turn the heat down to medium low and cook for a further 10 minutes, turning occasionally.

Meanwhile finely chop the stalks of the Swiss chard and add them to the pan with the beans. Roughly chop the leaves and add them to the pan for the last minute or two of cooking so as not to lose the flavor. Taste the beans and season with salt and pepper. Cook for a few more minutes if you want to achieve a thicker consistency. Divide the beans between four plates and lay a pork chop over each. Sprinkle over the reserved oregano leaves, finish with a drizzle of olive oil and serve.

NICE AND SIMPLE SPANISH GAZPACHO

Makes 8 tapas-sized (6 ounce) glasses or 4 bowls

- ¼ of a loaf (9 ounces) of yesterday's white bread
- 4 to 5 large ripe red tomatoes
- ¾ of a cucumber, peeled and roughly chopped
- 1 green pepper, deseeded and roughly chopped
- 2 cloves of garlic, peeled
- Spanish extra virgin olive oil
- sherry vinegar
- sea salt and freshly ground black pepper
- optional: a pinch of sugar
- optional garnishes: fresh soft herbs, red pepper, spring onion, Serrano ham or quail's eggs

On this trip I realized that those of us outside Spain have lost the point of this dish a bit. It's not about bright red cold soup in posh bowls - its roots are humble, authentic and wonderfully simple. The name "gazpacho" comes from "caspa" or "little piece" because, classically, this Spanish gem uses little bits of leftover bread to thicken the soup. It's worth mentioning that you'll need artisanal bread for this, as sliced processed bread won't behave the same when it's stale.

On my travels I discovered a speedy way of making this if you don't have time to let it chill in the fridge: layering up the ingredients over ice, then blitzing everything together for an instantly chilled result. I've peeled the tomatoes here, but if I'm feeling lazy I don't always bother. It won't affect the flavor, just the texture - so it's up to you really. It's great to get back to basics and rediscover this refreshing little appetizer.

Slice the bread, then cut off the crusts and put the bread into a bowl with ½ cup of water. Prick the top of each tomato with a small sharp knife, then drop them into a bowl and cover with boiling water. Leave for 30 seconds or so, then drain. Once they're cool enough to handle, take off their skins and get on with preparing the rest of the veg.

In your largest serving jug or a blender put your peeled tomatoes, chopped vegetables and cloves of garlic. Tip the soaked bread on top, then pour in a good lug or two of extra virgin olive oil and a small splash of sherry vinegar. Use an immersion blender to whiz all the layers together, or whiz in the blender. Once smooth, stop and have a taste. Add a pinch or two of salt and pepper and a good splash of water to loosen the mixture, whiz again, then have another taste to make sure you've got the right balance of salt, acid and freshness. Locals sometimes add a pinch of sugar for extra sweetness but if the tomatoes are really ripe you won't need to. It won't look as red as the gazpachos you might be used to seeing but that's OK, because the bread will turn it a pinky orange sort of color - which is authentic. Cover the jug of gazpacho with plastic wrap and put in the fridge to chill.

When the gazpacho is really cold, divide it between some little glasses or cups. Drizzle a little extra virgin olive oil on top and garnish with anything you fancy: fresh herbs, really delicately chopped peppers or onion, sliced Serrano ham, or even a hard-boiled quail's egg halved on top if you're feeling a bit fancy. Delicious, fresh and wonderfully simple.

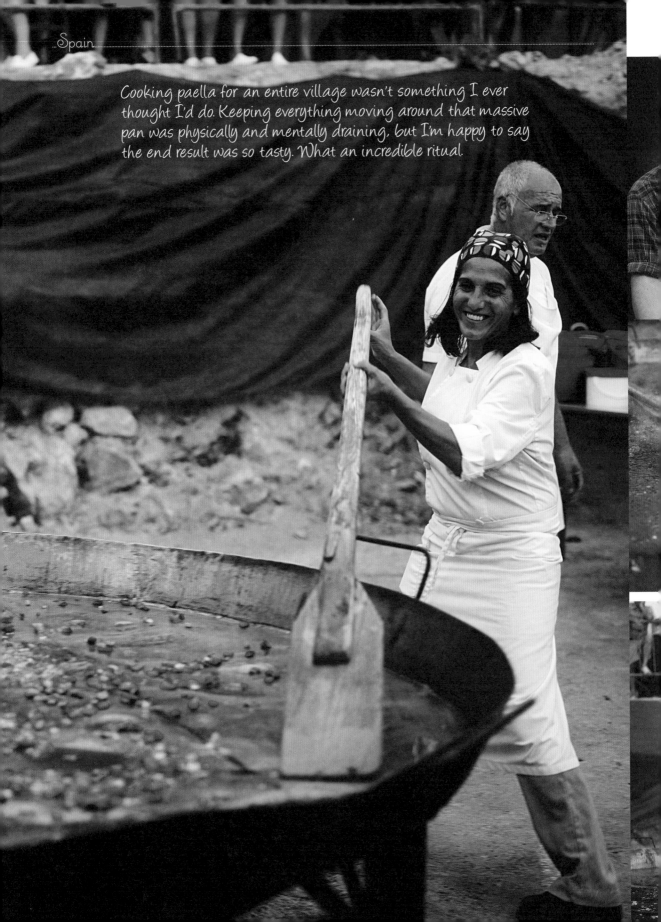

Cooking paella for an entire village wasn't something I ever thought I'd do. Keeping everything moving around that massive pan was physically and mentally draining, but I'm happy to say the end result was so tasty. What an incredible ritual.

MY FAVORITE PAELLA

Serves 4-6

- olive oil
- 2 raw chorizo sausages (approximately 9 ounces in total), thickly sliced
- 10½ ounces pork belly, skin removed, the best quality you can afford, cut into ⅓ inch pieces
- 1 green pepper, deseeded and roughly chopped
- 1 red pepper, deseeded and roughly chopped
- 5 cloves of garlic, peeled and roughly chopped
- 1 onion, peeled and roughly chopped
- a small bunch of fresh flat-leaf parsley, leaves picked and roughly chopped, stalks finely chopped
- sea salt and freshly ground black pepper
- a good pinch of saffron
- 14 ounces clams or mussels, scrubbed clean and debearded
- 2½ cups paella rice
- 7 ounce jar red peppers in oil, drained and torn into pieces
- 1 x 14 ounce can of chopped tomatoes
- 4⅓ cups chicken or vegetable stock, preferably organic
- 12 large shrimp, shells on
- 5½ ounces squid, cleaned and finely sliced
- 5½ ounces green beans, sliced very thinly at an angle
- 1 lemon, cut into wedges

As a young boy, the idea of meat and fish together in one dish never made sense to me. But once I tried paella the combination of textures and smoky flavors completely won me over. It's one harmonious, exciting, stomach-pleasing smasher of a dish. Some locals will say you don't add chorizo, but because I love it, I'm adding it here. You can pick up a proper paella pan (like the one in the picture) at most department stores, but a large shallow pan about 12 inches across will also work just fine.

Without question this is one of Spain's hero dishes. Although incredibly flexible and delicious, it was never intended to be as visual and flamboyant a dish as it is. It was invented by farmers, grabbing whatever bits of meat, veg and fish they had available to them and using rice to bring it all together. Over time it's been refined and claimed by all sorts of people around Spain as their own. That's the great thing about paella, you can make it your own by taking the principle of it and adjusting it to embrace whatever ingredients are in season and around you.

Heat a large wide-based pan over medium heat and add a lug of olive oil, the sliced chorizo and the pork belly. Fry for around 10 minutes, stirring occasionally. As soon as the chorizo starts taking on color and the fat is beginning to render, add the chopped peppers, garlic, onion and parsley stalks along with a good pinch of salt and pepper and the saffron. Fry gently for another 10 minutes, or until the vegetables have begun to soften. Meanwhile pick through the shellfish and get rid of any clams or mussels that aren't tightly closed.

Add the rice and jarred peppers and keep stirring for a few minutes until the rice is coated in all the lovely flavors, then pour in the canned tomatoes and 3¼ cups of stock, seasoning again with salt and pepper. Bring everything to the boil, then turn down to medium to low heat and stir constantly for about 15 minutes. This combination of flavors will be absolutely beautiful, but you've got to help the dish along by doing your job and making sure each grain of rice gets the same amount of love. So every now and then, stir from the outside of the pan into the middle so you get a sort of pile of rice in the center, making sure nothing is sticking to the bottom. Flatten the pile out with your spoon, then start the whole process again.

After 15 minutes the rice should be cooked, but still have a bit of a bite, so add the mussels or clams and the shrimp. You may want to add the extra splash of stock here if the rice looks a bit dry. Keep stirring, and as the clams and mussels start to open and the shrimp begin to turn pink, add your squid and green beans and cook for a further 5 minutes or so. Discard any clams or mussels that don't open. Stir in the chopped parsley leaves and the juice from half your lemon wedges, and bring to the table with the remaining lemon wedges on the side.

MI PESCADO A LA SAL
(MY FISH BAKED IN SALT)

Serves 2

For the fish

- 2 pounds kosher salt
- 2 large eggs, preferably free-range or organic
- 1½ tablespoons fennel seeds
- 1 lemon, peeled
- 1 x 1 pound 5 ounce sea bass or 2 portion-sized sea bass or dorade, gutted, scales left on, gills out (sustainably caught – see introduction)
- a small bunch of fresh basil
- a small bunch of fresh flat-leaf parsley

For the alioli

- 3 large cloves of garlic, peeled
- a pinch of saffron
- sea salt
- 3½ tablespoons olive oil
- 3½ tablespoons good-quality Spanish extra virgin olive oil

For the side salad

- ½ a cucumber, peeled
- a large handful of green olives, pitted
- 2 jarred red peppers
- a few sprigs of fresh flat-leaf parsley, leaves picked and chopped
- freshly ground black pepper

This Spanish technique of baking fish in a thick layer of salt is not only quite theatrical, it will also give you the most perfectly cooked fish ever. The salt is there to create a little kiln or oven around the fish so don't worry; you won't be eating any of it. Make sure the fish isn't scaled because the scales help keep the moisture inside the fish as it cooks. This is a great principle. Obviously sizes of fish and temperatures of ovens vary but as long as you keep an eye on things and test the fish before removing the salt, by inserting a knife into it and touching it to your lip, you should be just fine.

Preheat the oven as high as it will go. Put the kosher salt into a large, wide bowl with 2 tablespoons of water, your eggs, fennel seeds and the lemon peel. Mix everything together until clumpy, then spread two-thirds of the mixture in a roasting pan in a thick layer. Stuff the cavity of your fish with the basil and parsley (or any fragrant herbs), then lay the fish on the salt bed, and completely cover it with the rest of the salt so you get a layer just over ½ inch thick. Pat it down firmly, then put into the oven for 15 minutes.

Once cooked, remove from the oven, take a sharp knife and stick it through the salt into the middle of your fish. Carefully touch the knife to your lip and if it's hot, the fish is ready. Set aside for 10 minutes.

Meanwhile, pound and mush up the garlic, saffron and a good pinch of salt in a mortar and pestle until you've got a smooth, vibrant orange paste. Use the pestle to mix in the olive oil, a drizzle at a time. Be patient and wait until you've got a smooth emulsion before adding the next drizzle. Do the same with the extra virgin olive oil. If it separates, pour the mixture out, pound some more garlic and salt together, then really slowly add the mixture to that. Be patient! Go to www.jamieoliver.com/how-to if you want to see how it's done. Have a taste. Initially it will be fiery and you'll think you don't like it, but it's supposed to be that way. Add a squeeze or two of juice from your peeled lemon and taste again.

Roughly slice your cucumber and put it into a bowl. Tear the olives and add to the bowl along with the torn-up peppers, the parsley, a squeeze of lemon juice and a drizzle of extra virgin olive oil. Season with a little salt and pepper, then toss together.

By now the salt on your fish should be hard as a brick, so give it a whack around the edges with the back of a spoon, and if you're lucky, the whole top will peel off. Carefully brush the excess salt off your fish, trying not to let the salt touch the flesh, then gently move it to a platter using a fish spatula. Run a knife along the spine of the fish up to the head, then cut across the fish below the head. Use the knife to find the bones, then carefully lift the fillet up so the fish opens like a book. Discard the skin and bones and put beautiful big flakes of fish on your serving plates with a dollop of your alioli on top and some olive salad.

This year, for various reasons, I've found myself in situations where I've had to work around bulls. Speaking from personal experience, there are few things more frightening than having half a ton of pure power and muscle heading towards you. I was glad to see these kids using a pair of old horns on a wheelbarrow for their matador training rather than the real thing!

QUICK BREAKFAST OF QUAIL'S EGGS AND MORCILLA

Serves 2

- olive oil
- a few inches of morcilla (about 3½ ounces), roughly sliced
- Spanish extra virgin olive oil
- 4 quail's eggs
- 4 slices of baguette
- 2 cherry tomatoes, halved
- 4 slices of pata negra or Serrano ham
- sea salt and freshly ground black pepper
- optional: a few sprinkles of very finely sliced fresh red chile, to serve

I used to think quail's eggs were only for fancy picnics but the Spanish eat them all the time for their tapas, which gave me the idea for this breakfast. They're so sweet when used this way and they're tiny, so you can have a couple of them and not feel too greedy. Morcilla can be bought all over Spain, and also through websites like www.latienda.com. It's made with blood and pork fat, like the UK's black pudding, but the Spanish add other flavors which are much more interesting and varied: delicious stuff like cloves, cinnamon, paprika and a little oregano.

It might sound as if there's a lot going in here but actually, after you've made this once you'll get quicker and more efficient and things will be hot and lovely at the same time. So get in the groove and rattle this out.

Put a drizzle of olive oil into a small frying pan over medium heat and add your sliced morcilla. Fry for about 5 minutes, turning occasionally. When it's nice and crispy move it to some paper towels to drain. Run the pan under cold water then wipe it clean with paper towel. Drizzle in a little extra virgin olive oil. While the pan is off the heat, crack in the quail's eggs (they are sweet, but fiddly). Pop your slices of bread into the toaster, then put the pan of quail's eggs on the heat and fry for a minute or two, or until they're cooked to your liking. Tilt the pan and spoon some of the oil over the top of the eggs so they cook on top and become smooth and lovely.

When the toast pops up, rub the tomato halves over the toast for flavor and drizzle over some extra virgin olive oil. Arrange the toasts on a plate next to a little pile of crispy morcilla. Lay a slice of pata negra or Serrano ham on each toast, pop a cooked egg on top, then sprinkle over a pinch of salt and pepper and a few bits of finely sliced chile if you fancy. And there you go: a quick easy breakfast and four of the best mouthfuls in the world.

TAPAS

I love the story of tapas because it shows how the simplest of things can evolve into something wonderful with a life of its own.

When the old Spanish boys would be sitting around in the bars on a hot day, flies and mosquitoes would get into their drinks and just generally be a real pain in the backside. So they started putting covers on their glasses and jugs, and somewhere along the line some clever person started bringing out little hunks of cheese, bits of bread, and other delicious things to put on these covers and "tapas" were born. The word comes from the Spanish word "tapar," which means "to cover." It's now a big part of Spanish culture, and it's almost unheard of to go for a drink and not have a few things to eat because the two go hand in hand.

I think standing at a bar on a hot day with a drink and a few plates of tapas in front of you is one of the best things in the world. But as a chef, what I find most exciting is that no matter where you come from or what your budget is, you can easily capture the spirit of tapas, which is fun, buzzy and basically a party in your mouth. It doesn't matter if you don't have proper Spanish ingredients because you can take the heart and soul of tapas and apply it to whatever wonderful things you have near you. That could mean carved leftover ham, a few chunks of local cheese drizzled with lavender honey, tiny bits of fried fish with a few cloves of garlic, simple fried potatoes, mini Scotch eggs, even little slices of pork pie. It's about bright things, dark things, hot things, cold things, crunchy things, soft things, fish, meat, cheese, vegetables, leftovers ... the only rule is that there are no rules!

Just be adventurous and experimental with your ordering. If you don't like something, it's fine, because you haven't broken the bank, you can just move on and try something different. The one mistake people tend to make with tapas is ordering a load of them at once. The best thing to do is ask what's good, try a plate or two, then see how you feel after a few nibbles. But settle in for the duration, because it is a process and a pleasure that should be enjoyed.

CROQUETAS

Serves 4 as a tapas dish

- 3½ tablespoons butter
- 2 tablespoons Spanish extra virgin olive oil
- scant ⅔ cup all-purpose flour, plus an extra scant ½ cup for coating
- 1¼ cups milk
- sea salt and freshly ground black pepper
- ½ teaspoon freshly grated nutmeg
- 1½ ounces hard cheese, such as Manchego or Cheddar, finely grated
- 2 large slices of Serrano ham, roughly chopped
- vegetable oil
- 1 large egg, preferably free-range or organic
- scant ½ cup fine breadcrumbs

It's easy to confuse croquetas with their slightly sad cousin, the potato croquette. But let me assure you, Spanish croquetas are infinitely more exciting. They are filled with a creamy béchamel mixture that melts in your mouth when you take a bite. They are quite rich, you won't want more than one or two, which is why they make such a perfect tapa. I've mixed Manchego cheese and Serrano ham into my béchamel mixture because I think it gives these even more of a Spanish edge. Put a plate of these on any table and they'll be gone in a flash.

Melt the butter with the extra virgin olive oil in a large pan over low to medium heat. Once melted, stir in the ⅔ cup of flour, a spoonful at a time, waiting until it's well combined before adding the next spoonful. Keep going until you get a really thick paste and there's no more butter to soak up. Add your milk, a splash at a time, again stirring well each time so you've got a smooth mixture with no lumps. Once all the milk has been added, keep stirring and cooking for a minute or two until the mixture starts to really thicken. Season well to taste with a good pinch of salt and pepper, the grated nutmeg and the cheese. Take the pan off the heat, let the mixture cool, and stir in the chopped ham. Cover the pan with plastic wrap and put into the fridge for an hour so it can set.

Get three plates and put the beaten egg on one, the breadcrumbs on another and the flour on the last one. Add a pinch of salt and pepper to the ½ cup flour to season it. Dust some more flour over your hands, then take a large tablespoon of the chilled filling and mold it into a sausage shape, using your hands. As you go roll each of these in flour, then in beaten egg and breadcrumbs.

Fill a sturdy medium-sized pan about halfway with vegetable oil and put it on a high heat. Make sure you don't have any kids or pets running around the kitchen, as hot oil can burn badly. Drop a small piece of potato into the pan of oil. When it's golden and crisp and floats to the surface, the oil is ready. These croquetas are always best cooked in batches, so use a slotted spoon to carefully add about 4 or 5 at a time. Fry them for about 2 to 3 minutes, or until golden all over. Don't be tempted to add them when the oil isn't hot enough, because you'll find they melt and don't keep their shape. Move to some paper towel to drain, and serve right away, sprinkled with sea salt.

P.S. Feel free to experiment with different leftover meats, cheeses or mushrooms in the filling. Make it your own.

MINI MEATBALLS

Serves 4 as a tapas dish
(makes 12 small meatballs)

- olive oil
- a small bunch of fresh
  flat-leaf parsley
- 1 onion, peeled
  and finely chopped
- 2 cloves of garlic, peeled,
  1 finely chopped,
  1 finely sliced
- ½ pound ground beef or
  pork, the best quality you can
  afford (or a mixture)
- 1 large egg yolk, preferably
  free-range or organic
- 1½ tablespoons fine
  breadcrumbs
- sea salt and freshly ground
  black pepper
- 1 small dried chile
- 2 large ripe tomatoes
- 1 lemon
- Spanish extra virgin olive oil

I don't know what it is about meatballs, but every country seems to have its own take on them. Swedes serve them with gravy and berries, Americans put them in mini-buns and call them sliders and Italians toss them with spaghetti and tomato sauce. Everybody loves them! Serving a few meatballs as a snack, like they do in Spain, is a great idea, and including just a hint of lemon in the sauce helps freshen them up. They go down a treat with a cold beer or glass of wine.

Heat a lug of olive oil in a frying pan over medium heat. Finely slice the parsley stalks and add them to the pan with half your finely chopped onion. Fry the onion gently for a few minutes, and once it starts to soften, add the chopped garlic. Fry for a few more minutes, until the onion is completely softened, then put it into a large mixing bowl and leave to cool completely.

Once your onion has cooled, add the ground meat, egg yolk and breadcrumbs to the bowl. Roughly chop most of your parsley leaves and add to the bowl. Season well with salt and pepper, then crumble in the dried chile and use your clean hands to really get in there and scrunch everything up until well mixed. Roll the mixture into about 12 bite-sized balls, lay them on an oiled baking sheet, cover with plastic wrap and pop into the fridge to firm up for half an hour.

Although putting them into the fridge helps them hold their shape, if I'm rushed for time I'll often skip this step and take my chances. They may break up a little, but it's not the end of the world and they'll still taste delicious.

When the meatballs are ready get them out of the fridge. Prick the tomato a few times with a small sharp knife, then drop it into a bowl and cover with boiling water. Leave for 30 seconds or so, then use tongs to fish it out. Once it's cool enough to handle, peel and discard the skin, squeeze out the seeds and finely chop the flesh. Put a pan on high heat and add a lug of good olive oil. Add the meatballs and move them around for about 8 minutes, or until they are brown all over. Add the remaining chopped onion and the sliced garlic to the pan, fry for a couple of minutes, then add the chopped tomato and lemon. Shaking and stirring, simmer for around 5 minutes, or until everything looks beautiful and the onions are soft and cooked through. Halve your lemon and squeeze the juice from one half into the pan. Very finely chop a teaspoon's worth of lemon from the remaining half and add it to the pan.

Move everything to a serving dish, season with salt and pepper, drizzle over some extra virgin olive oil and scatter over the rest of the parsley leaves.

MANCHEGO

Serves 4 as a tapas dish

Slice a 4½ ounce hunk of **Manchego cheese** into wedges. Drizzle over 1 tablespoon of **runny honey** and serve with a couple of small sprigs of **fresh thyme** on top.

BLACKENED PADRÓN PEPPERS

Serves 4 as a tapas dish

Heat a large dry pan over medium to high heat. Once hot, add a splash of **olive oil** and about 20 **padrón peppers**. Cook them for about 15 minutes, turning occasionally, until slightly charred and blistered all over. Sprinkle over a good pinch of **sea salt** and serve.

STICKY PINE NUTS AND ARTICHOKES

Serves 4 as a tapas dish

Heat a lug of **olive oil** in a frying pan over medium heat. Peel thick strips from ¼ of a **lemon** and add them to the pan. Fry for a few minutes until crispy, add 2 sprigs of **fresh thyme**, then 3 tablespoons of **pine nuts**. Keep tossing and moving everything around in the pan, and as soon as the nuts start getting golden, drain a 10 ounce **jar of artichokes**.

Halve or quarter any larger ones, then add them all to the pan and cook until warmed through. Stir in 1 teaspoon of **honey**, season with a pinch of **sea salt** and **freshly ground black pepper**, and cook for a few more minutes until lovely and sticky. Move to a plate and dig in.

GRILLED ASPARAGUS

Serves 4 as a tapas dish

Preheat a grill pan over high heat for 5 minutes and let it get screaming hot. While that's happening snap the woody ends off a pound of **asparagus** and discard, then grill for 5 to 8 minutes, turning every now and then, so they start to get quite charred, nutty and delicious.

Meanwhile, bash a **garlic clove** in a mortar and pestle with a pinch of **sea salt** and **freshly ground black pepper**, then stir in the zest and juice of ½ a **lemon** and 3 times as much **Spanish extra virgin olive oil**. When the asparagus spears are charred and cooked, put them into a shallow bowl with your dressing to marinate for a few minutes. Transfer them to a plate and serve them with a handful of pitted **green olives** torn up over the top and your lemon zest sprinkled over.

CHORIZO AND GARLIC

Serves 4 as a tapas dish

Cut 5 ounces of **cooked chorizo sausage** into thick chunky slices. Add to a hot pan with a drizzle of **olive oil** and fry for 3 to 4 minutes, tossing occasionally. Once the chorizo is starting to look nice and crispy, add 4 peeled and roughly sliced **garlic cloves** and fry for a further minute, then take off the heat. Add 1½ tablespoons of **sherry vinegar** and a teaspoon of **honey**, stir everything around, then put the pan back on the heat for another minute to let everything caramelize. Transfer to a little bowl and drizzle over any juices from the pan. Serve with a hunk of bread and enjoy.

ANCHOVIES

Serves 4 as a tapas dish

Skewer 8 fillets of large good-quality **pickled anchovies** and arrange them on a pretty serving plate. Squeeze over the juice from ½ a **lemon**, then drizzle over a good lug of **Spanish extra virgin olive oil**. Hit them with a big pinch of **freshly ground black pepper**, scatter over a handful of roughly chopped **fresh flat-leaf parsley leaves**, then toss and put on a plate with some cocktail sticks.

SIMPLE EGGS AND HAM

Serves 4 as a tapas dish

- 2 large slices of Serrano ham, shredded
- olive oil
- 8 quail's eggs
- 1½ ounces hard goat's cheese, finely grated
- a couple of sprigs of fresh thyme, leaves picked
- freshly ground black pepper

These little eggs are really tiny and delicate, but they're also quite rich, which means you don't need to eat too many to feel full. Because they are so small it can be difficult to crack them without breaking the yolk or getting shell in the pan, so a nice little trick is to use a small sharp knife to pierce the top of the shell and the membrane underneath before cracking the eggs open. That little bit of effort is well worth it for the pretty results.

Fry your ham over medium heat in your smallest pan with a lug of olive oil until crisp. Crack your eggs into a bowl while you are waiting for the ham to cook. When the ham looks crispy, add your eggs to the pan and fry them for a couple of minutes more, or until the whites turn opaque. Sprinkle the cheese into the middle and let it start to melt, then scatter over the thyme leaves and a pinch of freshly ground black pepper, and tuck in.

P.S. If you wanted to make this with regular eggs in a larger pan it would work just as well. If you like your eggs cooked really well-done you could also finish this off under the broiler.

FRIED CHORIZO AND LENTILS

Serves 4 as a tapas dish

Fry 4 ounces of sliced **cooked chorizo sausage** for 2 minutes in a hot dry pan. When it starts getting crispy, drain a 14 ounce can **or jar of lentils** and add them to the pan. Heat them through for about a minute, adding a lug of **Spanish extra virgin olive oil** if it looks dry. Once hot, add a lug of **sherry vinegar** and another lug of oil. Stir through, then sprinkle over a handful of chopped **fresh flat-leaf parsley leaves** and serve.

MORCILLA

Serves 4 as a tapas dish

Slice 6 ounces of **morcilla** in half, then lengthways so you have 4 pieces. Get a frying pan nice and hot, then add a lug of **olive oil** and 4 unpeeled **cloves of garlic**. Cook for a few minutes, then add the morcilla slices and cook for another 4 minutes, turning occasionally, until the morcilla is nice and crispy. Transfer to a plate and drizzle over any juices from the pan. Simple.

SIMPLE GAMBAS

Serves 4 as a tapas dish

Fill a sturdy medium-sized pan about halfway with **vegetable oil** and put it over high heat. Make sure you don't have any kids or pets running around the kitchen, as hot oil can burn badly. Add a small piece of potato to the pan, and when it's golden and crisp and floats to the surface, the oil is ready, so carefully add 14 ounces of **small raw shrimp** with their shells on (sustainably caught – see introduction) – do this in a couple of batches so the oil stays hot and the shells go so crispy you can eat them. They won't take long to cook through, so after about 2 to 3 minutes, remove them with a slotted spoon to some kitchen paper to drain. Serve sprinkled with **sea salt** and a pinch or two of **paprika** and add a few **lemon wedges** on the side for squeezing over.

BABY CLAMS

Serves 4 as a tapas dish

Pick through 10 ounces of **small clams** (sustainably caught – see introduction) and get rid of any that aren't really tightly closed. Give them a good wash under a tap. Roughly chop the leaves from a few sprigs of **fresh flat-leaf parsley**. Preheat a frying pan large enough to hold all the clams over high heat and add a lug of **olive oil**. Roughly chop 2 **tomatoes** and add them to the pan along with the clams, 4 tablespoons of **good sherry** and a splash of **water**. Season with a pinch of **sea salt** and **freshly ground black pepper**, then toss and fry for 3 or 4 minutes, or until all the clams have opened (if any refuse to open, they're no good, so get rid of them). Sprinkle over the **chopped parsley** and serve right away.

CHORIZO AND CHICKEN LIVERS

Serves 4 as a tapas dish

Slice and peel 4 ounces of **cooked chorizo sausage** and finely slice 1 **onion**. Add a lug of **olive oil** to a hot pan and fry the chorizo and onion for 4 to 5 minutes, until the chorizo is crispy and the onions have softened. Add 4 whole **chicken livers** and fry for another 2 to 3 minutes until golden. Stir in 2 tablespoons of **sherry vinegar**, and use a wooden spoon to scrape all the lovely bits off the bottom of the pan. Spoon into a small serving dish, drizzling over any pan juices. Scatter over a handful of roughly chopped **fresh flat-leaf parsley** and serve.

SMASHED CHICKPEAS

Serves 4 as a tapas dish

Put a pan over medium heat and add a 14 ounce can of **chickpeas** and their juices. Boil for a few minutes, until the chickpeas are hot through, then take the pan off the heat and use a potato masher to mash them to a chunky consistency. Mix in 1 tablespoon of **sherry vinegar** and a lug or two of **Spanish extra virgin olive oil**. Peel a **clove of garlic** and finely grate or crush it into the mixture. Give everything a good stir and continue to cook to the consistency you like. Season with a good pinch of **sea salt**, then spoon on to a serving plate and drizzle over a little extra virgin olive oil. Sprinkle over the leaves from a few sprigs of **dried oregano** and a good pinch of **paprika**, and serve.

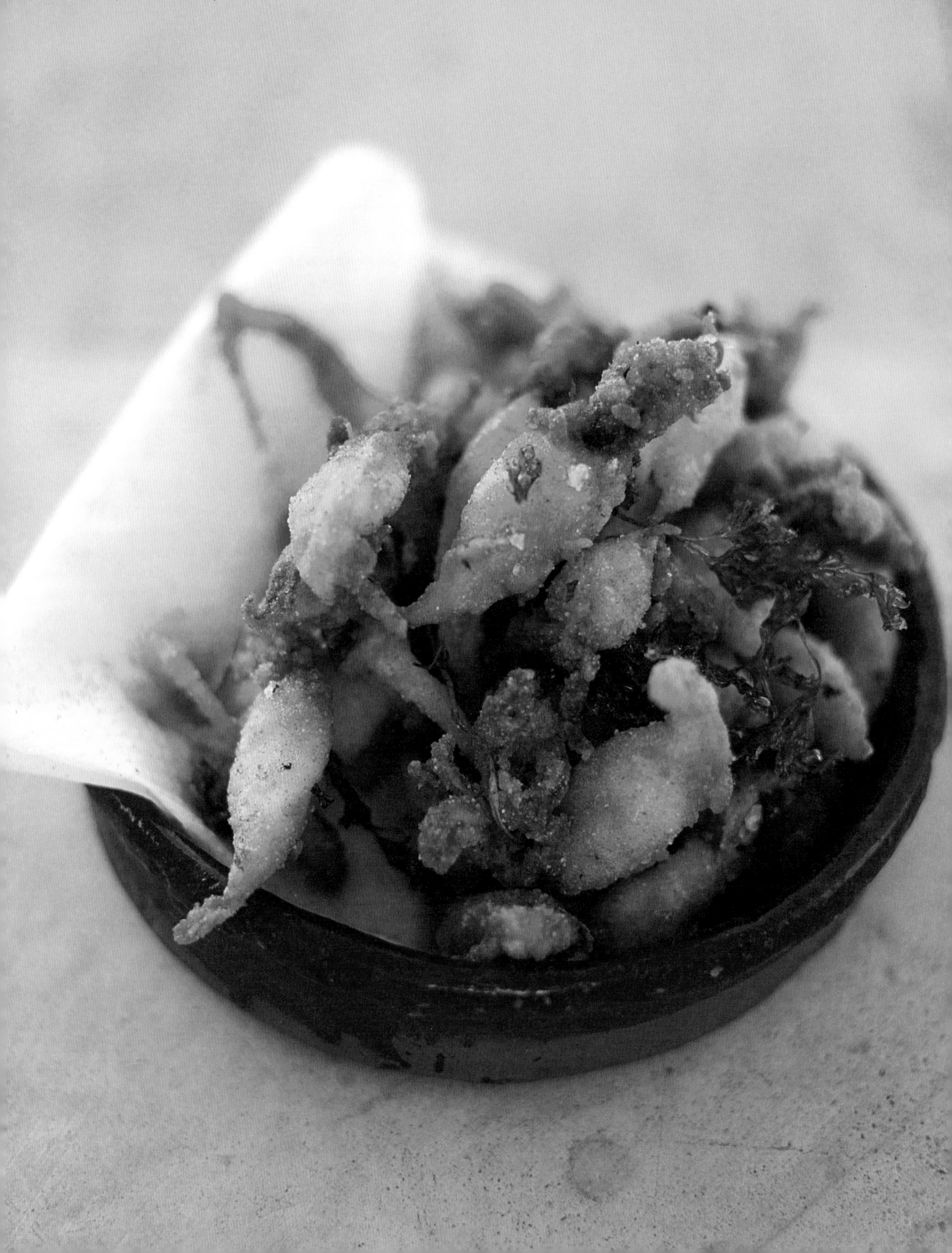

BABY SQUID

Serves 4 as a tapas dish

- ¾ cup all-purpose flour
- sea salt and freshly ground black pepper
- 10½ ounces whole baby squid, cleaned (sustainably caught – see introduction)
- vegetable oil
- 5 or 6 sprigs of fresh flat-leaf parsley
- hot smoked Spanish paprika
- 1 lemon, cut into wedges

Baby squid isn't as common in the US as it is in Spain, but regular squid sliced into smaller pieces will work just as well. The Spanish clean these little squid so cleverly they manage to leave them whole. And that means you get the best of both worlds in one mouthful: a soft squidgy top and crispy delicious tentacles (my favorite bit) on the bottom. If you're in a tapas bar and spot some of these, go for it.

Season the flour with a really good pinch of salt and pepper, then toss through the baby squid - if you're using regular squid, cut them in half lengthways and then into 2 inch triangles before you do this.

Fill a sturdy medium-sized pan about halfway with vegetable oil and put it over high heat. Make sure you don't have any young children or pets running around the kitchen, as hot oil can burn badly. Add a small piece of potato to the pan and when it's golden, crisp and floats to the surface, the oil is ready. Use a slotted spoon to lower the floured squid carefully into the pan in small batches, along with a few sprigs of parsley. Fry them for about 2 minutes, or until lightly golden and curling up, then remove them to a plate lined with paper towel to drain. Sprinkle each batch with a pinch of salt and smoked paprika as it comes out, and serve with lemon wedges on the side for squeezing over.

PATATAS BRAVAS

Serves 4 as tapas
- 4 medium potatoes, peeled and halved (approximately 1¾ pounds)
- 2 cloves of garlic, peeled and finely sliced
- 2 sprigs of fresh rosemary, leaves picked
- 1 teaspoon sweet paprika
- 1 teaspoon fennel seeds
- 1 teaspoon sea salt

For the bravas sauce
- olive oil
- 1 onion, peeled and finely chopped
- 4 cloves of garlic, peeled and sliced
- 3 fresh red chiles, deseeded and roughly chopped
- 1 carrot, peeled and finely chopped
- a few sprigs of fresh thyme, leaves picked
- 1 x 14 ounce can of chopped tomatoes
- 1 tablespoon sherry vinegar
- sea salt and freshly ground black pepper

Whether you're in Madrid or Manhattan, you'll have to look really hard to find a tapas bar that doesn't serve some version of these potatoes. They're beautiful fried simply with herbs and a pinch of salt, but even more exciting served in a spicy tomato "bravas" sauce. "Patatas bravas" actually means "fierce potatoes" ... How could anyone resist something with such a brilliant name?

Parboil the potatoes over medium heat for 10 to 15 minutes, or until they are starting to get tender but still hold their shape. Drain in a colander and leave to steam dry until cool.

Meanwhile, put a pan over low heat and start your bravas sauce. Add a lug of olive oil and, once hot, add the chopped onion and sliced garlic. Cook for 5 minutes, or until the onion is soft but not colored. Add the chiles, carrot and thyme leaves and cook for another 5 minutes. Add the canned tomatoes, sherry vinegar and a good pinch of salt and pepper. Bring to a boil, then turn the heat down and simmer for 15 minutes, or until the carrots are soft and the sauce is lovely and thick.

While your sauce simmers, put a large frying pan over medium heat and add enough olive oil to cover the bottom of the pan by ¼ inch. Cut your potatoes into large bite-sized chunks. Once the oil is hot, carefully add your potatoes to the pan. Cook them for around 8 minutes, turning occasionally, until golden all over. You'll need to do this in batches so you don't overcrowd the pan. Add your garlic and rosemary leaves to the pan for the last minute of cooking.

Transfer the potatoes, garlic and rosemary to a plate lined with paper towels to drain, then scatter over the paprika, fennel seeds and a good pinch of salt and toss together until well coated.

Carefully tip your cooked sauce into a blender, or use an immersion blender, and whiz until lovely and smooth. Have a taste, and adjust the seasoning if necessary. Serve in a jug next to your potatoes or, if you want to be more traditional, pour the sauce over your potatoes before serving and toss together like I've done here. If you have any leftover sauce, use it with pasta or on a homemade pizza.

TORTAS DE ACEITE (INCREDIBLE OLIVE OIL BISCUITS)

Makes 12 crackers

- 1⅓ cups Italian Tipo 00 or cake flour
- 1 teaspoon sea salt
- 2 teaspoons fennel seeds
- Spanish extra virgin olive oil
- 3 tablespoons raw sugar, plus extra for sprinkling
- 2 teaspoons active dry yeast
- confectioners' sugar, for dusting
- all-purpose flour, for dusting
- 1 large egg white, preferably free-range or organic, beaten

Most people in Spain tend to buy their pastries and cakes rather than make them. I was told that the local nunnery was the place to go, so I headed there. The nuns were hidden from view behind a shuttered window and after a hilarious conversation with one of them I passed my money through a gap in the wall and lo and behold – the most beautiful little cakes and pastries appeared like magic.

My favorites were these thin little "tortas de aceite," or olive oil biscuits, which the nuns were also calling "tortas del virgin." You'll be able to buy these in good food shops here, but I think it's quite nice to recreate them at home with this slightly healthier biscuit recipe.

Preheat your oven to 450°F. Mix your flour, salt and fennel seeds in a bowl. Pour a scant ½ cup extra virgin olive oil into a jug with ⅔ cup warm water, then add the raw sugar and yeast and mix well. Leave for a few minutes.

Make a well in the center of the flour mixture and slowly pour in the yeast mixture, using a fork to gradually mix in the flour from the outside as you go. When it all starts to come together, use your hands to mix it into a lovely smooth dough.

Lightly oil two large baking sheets, then dust them with confectioners' sugar. Lightly flour a clean work surface and a rolling pin. Divide your dough into 12 equal-sized pieces and roll each one into a ball, then roll out each ball until it's about 4 inches in diameter. Put these on your trays, and brush each one with some beaten egg white. Dust each biscuit lightly with confectioners' sugar so they all have an even coating, and scatter over a little raw sugar.

Bake in the hot oven for around 10 to 12 minutes, or until golden and crisp. Transfer to wire racks to cool, then tuck in.

TINTO DE VERANO SORBET

Serves 6
- 2½ cups sugar
- 1¼ cups Spanish red wine, such as Rioja
- 1¼ cups lemon-flavored soda
- zest and juice of 1 lemon

The Spanish make absolutely beautiful wines and although they take good wine seriously, they also know how to have fun with ... how can I say this? ... less-good wine. I promised the new friends I made on this trip that I'd try a tinto de verano cocktail before I left. Imagine my surprise when I found out that the cold, refreshing and delicious cocktail I'd been enjoying was a mixture of cheap red wine and lemon soda!

Even though it was an unexpected combo, the flavors really worked together. So I've decided to turn their beloved cocktail into something even sweeter, and more refreshing. I've used a slightly better quality of wine for a deeper flavor and I think this is an absolutely gorgeous dessert. Tell your guests the recipe is based on a mysterious Spanish cocktail. They'll never guess the secret.

Heat 1¼ cups of water and the sugar in a pan over medium heat until the sugar dissolves. Turn the heat up and bring it up to a rapid boil to thicken the syrup, removing it from the heat after about 5 to 7 minutes, before it starts to color. Put it aside to cool.

Pour the red wine and soda into a large jug and add the lemon zest and juice. Add the cooled syrup to the mixture and give it a good stir. At this point you have two choices: you can pour it into a large deep tray, cover that with plastic wrap and put it into the freezer for a few hours, chuffing it up with forks every 15 minutes for the first hour then leaving it until completely frozen, or you can divide it between a few Tupperware containers and freeze those. It all depends whether you want to eat it all that day, or have smaller portions on hand for quick desserts.

Either way, before serving, tip the frozen sorbet into a food processor in small batches and quickly blitz until light, fluffy and delicate. Serve with fresh fruit and a sprig or two of fresh mint if you like.

JAMÓN

The Spanish take their *jamón*, or ham, extremely seriously and use time-honored artisan methods of production. The finest is *jamón Ibérico* or *pata negra*, which means "black foot." The black-footed pigs it comes from feed on acorns and herbs outside and their rich diet gives the meat its distinctive flavor. Hams are salted and dried in underground cellars, then hung. The curing process can take anywhere from 12 to 36 months.

ANCHOVIES

Anchovies are small saltwater fish sold fresh or preserved. Fresh fillets marinated in a mixture of olive oil, vinegar and herbs are called *boquerones* and are served as a tapa throughout Spain. Canned, preserved anchovies are called *anchoas*. They are hand-filleted and are either covered with olive oil or sunflower oil before sealing.

PAPRIKA

La Vera in Extremadura, Central Spain, is home to the best **paprika** in Spain, *pimentón de La Vera*. Various kinds of peppers are smoke-dried over oak wood, then pounded to a fine powder of varying degrees of heat. Paprika is used to flavor everything from chorizo and paella to soups and stews.

GREEN OLIVES

Spanish **olives** come in many varieties, including *arbequina* and *hojiblanca*, both of which produce some of the finest Spanish olive oils. They are often served as tapas stuffed with anchovies and red pepper. They can be bought in jars in good specialty markets.

CHEESE, MEMBRILLO AND CRACKERS

The most famous of the **Spanish cheeses** are *manchego*, a hard sheep's cheese, *cabrales*, an artisan blue cheese made from cow's milk, and a wide variety of goat's cheeses ranging from hard to creamy. Cheese, especially *manchego*, is often served as a tapa with *membrillo*, a quince paste.

Tortas de aceite are thin and crispy biscuits made with olive oil. They are healthier than other traditional pastries, and are often flavored with almonds and anise and topped with crystallized sugar. Delicious served with cheeses (see recipe on page 58).

PIMIENTOS DE PIQUILLO

Small dark red **peppers** that are grilled over fire once harvested, then skinned, seeded, hand-packed and preserved in cans or jars. They can be stuffed with salt cod or cheese and served as a tapa, or simply torn up into salads, paella or other rice dishes.

CHORIZO, CHICKPEAS AND PAELLA RICE

Chorizo is the national sausage of Spain and comes in all sorts of different shapes and sizes, raw or cured, spicy or even sweet. It is made from lean pork and fat and seasoned with garlic, salt, paprika and sometimes wine.

Chickpeas or **garbanzo beans** are a staple in most Spanish soups and stews, as are lentils and other bean varieties. They are very high in protein.

The best **paella rice** comes from Calasparra in Valencia. Paella rice is similar in texture and behavior to Italian risotto rice. Mainly used for Spain's national dish, paella.

I
ITALY

ITALY

Time and time again my trips to Venice would be cancelled at the last minute. It seemed ridiculous that this city I'd always wanted to visit kept escaping me, so this time I made sure it happened. It's no secret that my heart belongs to Italy.

Everything about the country, from the food to the way people live life there, has always felt like home to me. So, in a way, that made Venice the odd one out in this book because I already knew the food there so well. It was like knowing a language without ever having visited the country. Even so, the city still had so many wonderful surprises up its sleeve.

Although we've probably all seen James Bond movies, *The Italian Job*, and paintings and pictures of the city, nothing can quite prepare you for being surrounded by water and boats the way you are in Venice. It's a destination that has fascinated the rest of the world for centuries, and rightly so, because a lagoon in the Adriatic Sea is one of the last places you'd expect to find a city like this. But there it is, sitting on the water on the same wooden piles it's been sitting on for hundreds of years. The people who settled the islands in the fifth century AD were running away from Barbarian invasions on the mainland. Eventually they decided to drill wooden piles down into the bed of the lagoon and make rafts they could build on. How they managed to figure it out and actually make it happen, I can't imagine, but they made it work for them in the most incredible way. It's truly amazing to me that the architecture could achieve what it has. By the Middle Ages, Venice was its own Republic, a major trading center and one of the wealthiest places in the world.

If I had to sum up Venetian food, I would say that it's a cuisine of contrasts. On the one hand, you've got exceptionally luxurious food that would have had its origins in the kitchens of the rich: dishes that use fancy spices from distant lands, fine wine, incredible game from the marshes and seafood galore from the waters all around the city. There is definitely a flamboyance and elegance to the food, and squid ink, which Venetians use in pastas and risottos, is a great example of that. It's as black as your hat. You'd never think something so strangely dark could be so damn delicious, but it is.

Of course the flip side to all that luxurious food is the humble, honest, down-to-earth cooking done by the majority of people. Venice went through some tough, dark times when it lost its superpower status, and even rich nobles had to get used to, and fall in love with, "cucina povera," or poor people's cooking. But, as most people who love food will tell you, this style of cooking is often just as exciting, if not more so, than posh food. A great example of this is risotto, one of Venice's most famous dishes. The paddy fields in the Veneto region mean risotto rice is abundant, and cheap. Risotto is, and has always been, one of my favorite things to cook, so spending time in a city famed for this oozy, warming dish was a real dream for me. Without a doubt, one of the highlights for me was cooking with risotto-maker extraordinaire Signor Ruggero, who is famous for being one of the best risotto cooks in all of Italy. What an honor. I like to think making risotto is something I am fairly skilled at, but after such great mentoring, who knows, perhaps the risottos on pages 84–87 will be my best ones ever!

Because I didn't have long, I jumped right into the mix. I went fishing and cooked with the locals, I stopped by tiny allotments along the canals where people were growing the most ridiculous array of fruits and vegetables, I shopped at markets that have been part of city life for hundreds of years and I even visited a vegetable garden in the women's prison! These were all fantastic experiences, where, although I already knew the food, I was able to get that little bit closer to understanding it completely.

As this chapter proves, there was loads of great food to be discovered. But as with any city that attracts so many tourists, Venice has almost evolved to please those tourists. From talking to some of the locals, I got the feeling that a lot of them were nervous that their quirky Venetian food was getting squeezed out in favor of more generic Italian dishes. So my advice is to go where they go, and eat what they eat. Don't ask for dishes that have nothing to do with Venice! Embrace the city for what it is: a place to express genius. There are so many beautiful things to eat, see and enjoy. The charm of the place really is phenomenal.

No matter what anyone says, I can't believe Venice will sink into the lagoon one day. Just like their ancestors found amazing ways to build the city, I'm sure the Italians will find new and clever ways to prop up those homes and national treasures. There's no denying that the elements play a big role in everyday Venetian life: the city is flooded on a regular basis, and when weather comes in, it comes in quick. But in a funny way, the fact that the city is a little bit fragile and a little bit vulnerable just helps you appreciate it even more for the special place it is.

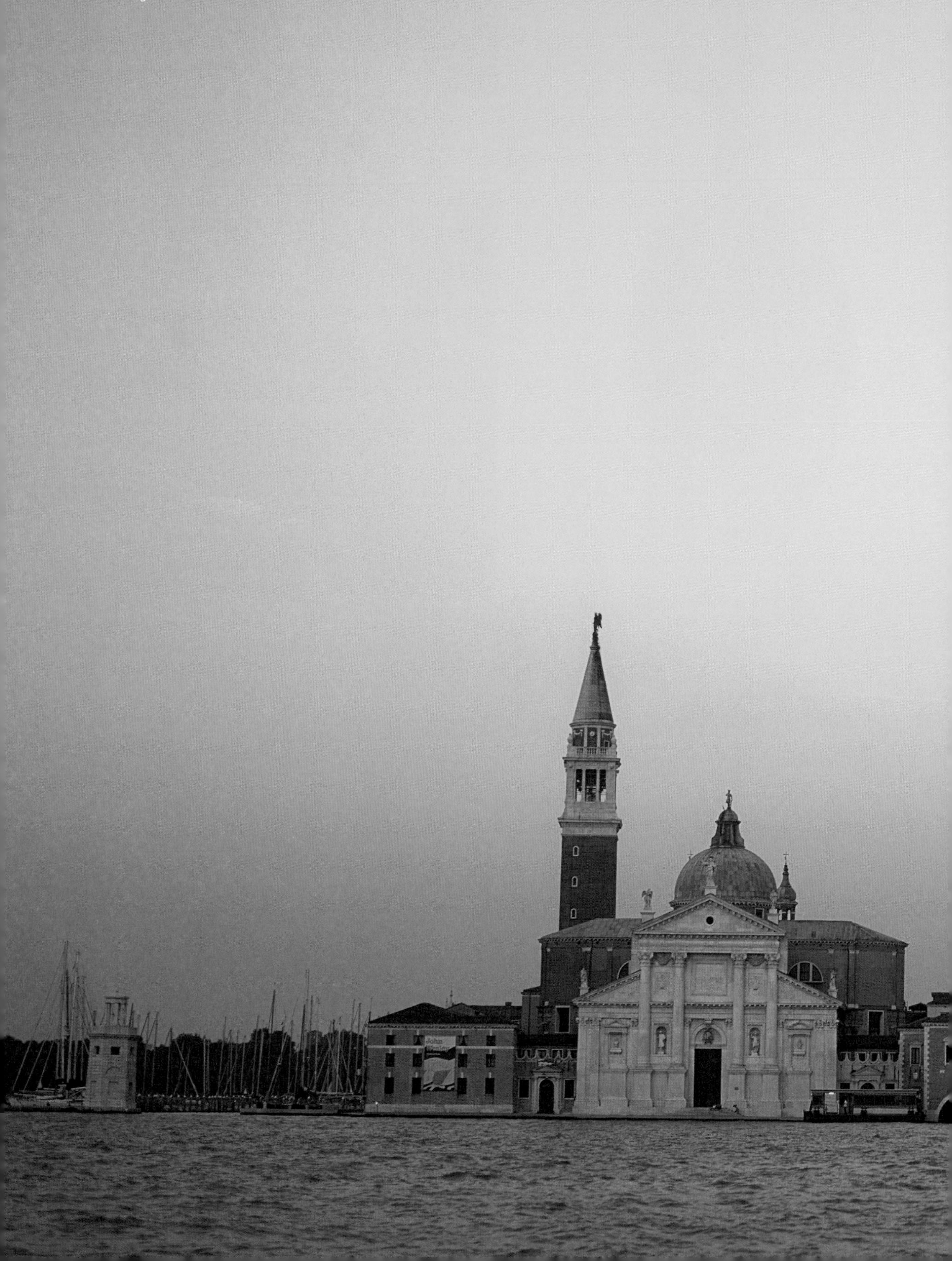

CARPACCIO AND SALAD

Serves 6 as a starter

- 1 x 10½ ounce good beef fillet or tenderloin, fat trimmed off
- ½ a lemon
- extra virgin olive oil
- sea salt and freshly ground black pepper
- 2 baby zucchini, with flowers if you can get them
- ½ a stick of celery, leaves reserved
- a few leaves of radicchio or endive, shredded
- a handful of arugula leaves
- a couple of sprigs of fresh mint, leaves picked and roughly chopped
- optional: ½ a fresh red chile, finely chopped
- Parmesan cheese, to serve

As carpaccio was invented in Harry's Bar, in Venice, it feels right to pay homage to this modern-day classic here. The story goes that back in the day, one of the bar's regular customers could only eat raw meat. The owner of the bar, Giuseppe Cipriani, decided to help her out and invented this now legendary dish. Inspired by a famous Venetian artist, Carpaccio, who always used pinks and whites in his work, Giuseppe splattered a white dressing over his raw pink beef and named it after the artist. The original recipe is so simple, so humble, that it's almost unimpressive. But because it works so well, versions of this dish have appeared in good restaurants around the world. Pretty phenomenal!

Some people pull faces and feel uncomfortable when they think of eating thin slices of raw meat, but if you have great fresh meat it's actually much easier to eat and digest than when it's cooked. I think this is a pleasure to eat and tastes amazing, so give it a chance. If you want to add a heaped teaspoon of Dijon mustard to the dressing to make it a bit more like the classic, go for it. Personally, I prefer the simplicity of lemon juice and olive oil, so that's what I've done here.

Slice the tenderloin evenly into 6 slices. Get yourself a large piece of plastic wrap and put a slice of beef on it. Fold the paper over so the meat is covered, then put it on a chopping board and bash it with the bottom of a pan or a rolling pin until it's really evenly thin. When it has doubled in size, hold it up to the light: if you can see some light coming through it, it's perfect. Repeat with all your slices, then arrange them on a large platter and spread them right out to the edges.

Squeeze your lemon juice into a large bowl and add roughly the same amount of extra virgin olive oil. Season well with salt and pepper and mix together. Lightly drizzle half this dressing over the beef and gently rub it around with the back of the spoon.

To make your salad, tear the zucchini flowers, if you have them, into the bowl of dressing. Use a peeler to peel your zucchini and celery into ribbons, straight into the bowl. Add the radicchio or endive, arugula, mint leaves and chile, if using, and toss everything together quickly with your hands. Scoop it all up and put it in the middle of the beef. Shave over a few slivers of Parmesan, and finish with a drizzle of extra virgin olive oil and any reserved celery leaves.

STUFFED ZUCCHINI FLOWERS

Serves 4

- a bunch of mixed fresh soft herbs, such as basil, mint, flat-leaf parsley and chervil
- 8 ounces good-quality ricotta
- 3½ tablespoons freshly grated Parmesan cheese
- ground nutmeg
- sea salt and freshly ground black pepper
- 1 lemon
- 12 large zucchini flowers or 16 small ones, baby zucchini left attached
- 1 pound ripe vine tomatoes
- olive oil
- 2 cloves of garlic, peeled and sliced
- 3 small banana (long) shallots, peeled and finely chopped
- a handful of black olives, stones removed
- extra virgin olive oil
- crusty bread and salad, to serve

One of the most exciting things about zucchini is their flowers; not just their sweet, polleny, floral flavors, but the fact that they can be stuffed with all sorts of wonderful things. If you don't grow your own, zucchini flowers can be a little hard to get hold of, but between July and late September most allotments, markets and farms will have them coming out of every nook and cranny, so beg or barter until you get some. I used male zucchini flowers the day I made this recipe; female zucchini have flowers attached to the end of the vegetable. You can use either, or a mixture if you like.

The moral of this story is that if you have a combo that works, from chile, fennel seeds and pork, to lemon, fennel and picked crab, to different cheeses and herbs – whatever you genuinely think is a beautiful thing – you should stuff some into the flowers, then roast, steam, bake or fry them … In this recipe I've created a delicious basic tomato sauce, which I then half steamed and half stewed the flowers in for ten minutes. It was a total reflection of Venice on the day that I was there. I wasn't sure whether to eat it out of the pan, spoon it over bruschetta or hack it up like a heathen and toss steaming hot pasta through it, but by the time I'd stopped arguing with myself about how to eat it, I'd eaten it.

Pick the leaves off your bunches of herbs, then finely chop them and the tender stalks. Place them in a bowl with the ricotta, Parmesan, a pinch of nutmeg and a pinch of salt and pepper, then finely grate in the zest of your lemon. Mix well with a fork, then have a taste and check the seasoning. Very carefully open up the zucchini flowers, keeping them attached to the zucchini, and snip off the pointed stamen inside. Gently rinse the flowers, then carefully fill each one with a generously heaped teaspoon of the ricotta mixture. Carefully press and pat the petals back together to seal in the mixture.

Cut a small cross in the top and bottom of your tomatoes. Plunge them into a bowl of boiling water for a minute or so until their skins start to come away. Place in cold water until cool enough to handle, then peel the skin off and discard. Cut the flesh into ½ inch chunks. In a wide pan, heat a good lug of olive oil over medium heat and fry the garlic and shallots for 3 to 4 minutes, until soft. Add the tomatoes and olives and bring to the boil, then season with salt and pepper and simmer over medium heat for 5 minutes, until thickened slightly.

When your sauce is ready, carefully lay your stuffed zucchini flowers on top and drizzle them with extra virgin olive oil. Pop the lid on the pan or cover with foil, and leave on a low heat to simmer for 15 to 20 minutes, until the zucchini are cooked through and the sauce is lovely and thick. Cut your zested lemon in half – squeeze one half into the sauce and cut the remaining half into wedges to serve. Tear your crusty bread into chunks and serve on the side for mopping up all the juices.

CRISPY CURED MEAT AND CHERRY SALAD

Serves 4-6 as a starter

- 2 large handfuls of mixed salad leaves, such as radicchio, frisée and little gem lettuce, baby leaves left whole, larger leaves torn into pieces, washed and spun dry
- a large handful of dark ripe cherries, pitted and torn
- a bunch of mixed fresh soft herbs, such as chervil, mint, flat-leaf parsley, dill and fennel tops, leaves picked
- optional: edible flowers
- a small loaf of ciabatta, cut into about 12 slices
- extra virgin olive oil
- olive oil
- 10 slices of pancetta, prosciutto, salami or a mixture
- 1 tablespoon good-quality balsamic vinegar
- sea salt and freshly ground black pepper
- optional: freshly grated Parmesan, to serve

Anyone who loves salads knows that reacting to seasons and what's available means that you always want to eat them, because they're exciting, fun and tasty. This recipe was based around the idea of contrast and best friends: sweet, slightly sour cherries with salty crispy pancetta, a mixture of crunchy, soft and bitter summer leaves, and a straightforward balsamic dressing. Basically it's a regular salad but I've been bothered to bust open some cherries and crisp up some pancetta - it's like a carnival in your mouth!

Place a grill pan over high heat and a frying pan over medium heat. While they are heating up, tip your salad leaves into a bowl with the pitted cherries, soft herbs and edible flowers, if using. Toast your ciabatta slices on the really hot grill pan until gorgeous and charred on both sides. Drizzle with extra virgin olive oil, then put aside. While your bread is toasting, pour a little oil into the frying pan and fry your cured meat for a couple of minutes on each side until crispy. Make the salad dressing in a small glass or jam jar while your meat fries. Mix the balsamic vinegar with 3 tablespoons of extra virgin olive oil and a good pinch of salt and pepper. Taste it and make sure it's slightly too acidic with a really nice flavor.

When your meat is nice and crispy, get it out of the pan and on to a plate. Pour the dressing into the pan and swirl it around for 10 seconds or so to let it warm slightly and mingle with the juices from the meat. Break the slices of toast up and either add them to the salad or arrange on a platter.

Add the meat to the bowl of salad, then drizzle over the warmed dressing from the pan and toss really quickly before serving. Beautiful with a few gratings of freshly grated Parmesan.

I had the pleasure of cooking with Italy's finest risotto cook, Signor Ruggero, at his restaurant, Trattoria al Gatto Nero, on the island of Burano outside Venice. Everything that came out of the kitchen was beautifully cooked and full of pride. We only cooked together for a day, but he was a lovely, fatherly man and we had great banter going on between us: the young cook and the wise cook. To make things even more surreal, his very Italian son was married to a Glaswegian girl. His English was spot-on Glaswegian, but in the body of the most Italian Italian. Hilarious!

RISOTTO BIANCO

Serves 4

- 4⅓ cups vegetable stock, preferably organic
- olive oil
- ½ an onion, peeled and finely chopped
- 1 stick of celery, trimmed and finely chopped
- 2½ cups risotto rice
- sea salt and freshly ground black pepper
- ½ cup white wine
- a knob of butter
- a large handful of freshly grated Parmesan cheese

Risotto is one of the stars of Venetian cuisine, thanks to all the rice paddies in and around the Veneto. There are two types of risotto: arborio and carnaroli. I've had good results with both but I think really it's about massaging out the best of the flavors as it cooks. Without sounding too soppy, a well-made risotto is like a big cuddle from your mum: it just makes you feel good. Life is far too short not to know how to nail it properly, so I really want you to use the versions of risotto on this and the next page to help you get your head around the principles. Master the mother recipe, then use your common sense, feel the power and create your own take on it. I've given you a few of my favorite flavors on the next page to get you started, but feel free to let your imagination run wild!

Pour your stock into a pan and leave on low heat. Get an appropriately high-sided pot on low heat and add a good lug of olive oil, the chopped onion and the celery. Cook gently for 10 minutes, stirring occasionally, until soft but not colored. Turn the heat up to medium, add the rice and a pinch of salt and stir for 2 minutes, so that the rice sucks up all the lovely flavor and develops a nutty taste. Pour in the wine and stir until absorbed.

Add a ladleful of hot stock, stir, and wait until it's been fully absorbed before adding more. Cook for 16 to 17 minutes, adding more stock every minute or so and stirring regularly, until the rice is al dente. This means it should be soft and a pleasure to eat, but still holding its shape. At this stage the risotto should be slightly looser than you want it to be finally, as it will thicken as it sits. Take the pan off the heat, stir or beat in the butter and Parmesan, then season to taste. At this point you've got an absolutely delicious risotto bianco, which is simple, lovely comfort food. You can either tuck in, or you can take it a few steps further by adding different cheeses or vegetables. Once you've taken it as far as you want, pop the lid on and let it sit for 2 minutes before serving. The most important thing to keep in mind is that risotto must always be oozy, or "all 'onda" (on the wave), as Signor Ruggero likes to say. He's the risotto master, so he really knows what he's talking about.

To flavor your basic risotto bianco, make your chosen flavoring as your rice is cooking ...

ARTICHOKE RISOTTO

Serves 4

- 2 lemons
- 8 baby artichokes
- olive oil
- 2 cloves of garlic, peeled and finely sliced
- a very small bunch of fresh thyme, leaves picked
- Parmesan cheese
- extra virgin olive oil

Prep the artichokes before you even start the risotto bianco. Squeeze the juice of 1 lemon into a big bowl of cold water, then add the squeezed halves. Trim the stalk off each artichoke about 1½ inches from the base (if long), and slice the top 1½ inches off the head. Quickly click back the outer leaves to reveal the tender leaves beneath. Peel the stalk and the base with a knife and a peeler, and right away dunk the artichoke in the lemon water to stop it going black. Cut it in half, use a teaspoon to get rid of the furry "choke" in the center and any fluffy bits, then put back in the water. Repeat until all your artichokes are done.

Heat a pan over medium heat and add a generous lug of olive oil and the garlic. Cook for 2 minutes, until soft. Finely slice the artichokes, and add to the pan with half the thyme leaves, a pinch of salt and pepper, a splash of water and the juice of half your remaining lemon. Cook for 8 to 10 minutes, or until softened. As you're finishing the risotto bianco with butter and Parmesan, add the remaining thyme leaves and the tasty artichokes. Put the lid on the pan for 2 minutes, then serve with some grated Parmesan, a drizzle of extra virgin olive oil and lemon wedges for squeezing over.

TOMATO AND BASIL RISOTTO

Serves 4

- olive oil
- 2 cloves of garlic, peeled and finely sliced
- 10½ ounces cherry tomatoes, halved
- a couple of sprigs of fresh basil, leaves picked
- Parmesan cheese
- extra virgin olive oil

Heat a lug of olive oil in a large pan over medium heat. Add the garlic, and as soon as it starts to lightly color, add the tomatoes and most of the basil leaves. Season with salt and pepper and cook gently for 3 minutes, until the tomatoes are soft but still holding their shape. As you're finishing the risotto bianco with the butter and Parmesan, stir in the lovely tomatoes, then pop the lid on the pan for 2 minutes. Serve with some grated Parmesan on top, a drizzle of extra virgin olive oil and the reserved basil leaves scattered over.

PEA AND HERB RISOTTO

Serves 4

- a knob of butter
- 1¼ cups fresh or frozen peas
- a small bunch of fresh mint, leaves picked and chopped
- a small bunch of fresh flat-leaf parsley, leaves picked and chopped
- 3½ ounces soft goat's cheese
- Parmesan cheese
- extra virgin olive oil

Melt the butter in a pan over medium heat and add the peas, fresh herbs and a splash of hot water. Put the lid on and cook for 4 minutes. As you're finishing the risotto bianco with butter and Parmesan, stir in the herby peas, then put the lid back on the pan for 2 minutes. Divide between your plates and pop a slice of goat's cheese in the center of each portion. Serve with some grated Parmesan and a drizzle of extra virgin olive oil.

TOMATO AND
BASIL SALAD

Serves 2
- 2 large ripe beefsteak tomatoes
- a small bunch of fresh basil or purple basil
- sea salt and freshly ground black pepper
- 5 tablespoons extra virgin olive oil
- 2 tablespoons red wine vinegar
- a small chunk of salted ricotta or feta cheese
- crusty bread, to serve

Caprese, tricolore ... how many times can we reinvent tomato salad? I guess this is a version of those classics, just done my way. In the last forty years, we've been given an edited variety of tomatoes. But the truth is that there are hundreds of them out there: fat, thin, ugly, pretty, tasty, sweet, yellow, peardrop, tiger-skin, black ... the options are endless. But my favorite are beefsteak tomatoes. These big babies are sweet, dense and absolutely delicious when they are ripe. Because they are bigger I like to treat them simply, so I just put four best friends together – tomato, basil, salty cheese and good olive oil – in a way that helps you get all those flavors in each bite.

Cut your tomatoes horizontally into thick slices, and divide between two plates or a platter. Pick your basil leaves, keeping the smaller ones to one side, then use a pestle and mortar to bash the rest to a pulp with a pinch of salt until you have a thick green paste. Gradually add the extra virgin olive oil and red wine vinegar, stirring with the pestle as you go, to make a lovely thick basil oil. Taste and season, then spoon simply over the tomatoes using the back of the spoon to smear it all around. Crumble or finely grate over a small hunk of ricotta or feta cheese. Place the reserved baby basil leaves in the middle and enjoy served with hot bread ... Delicious!

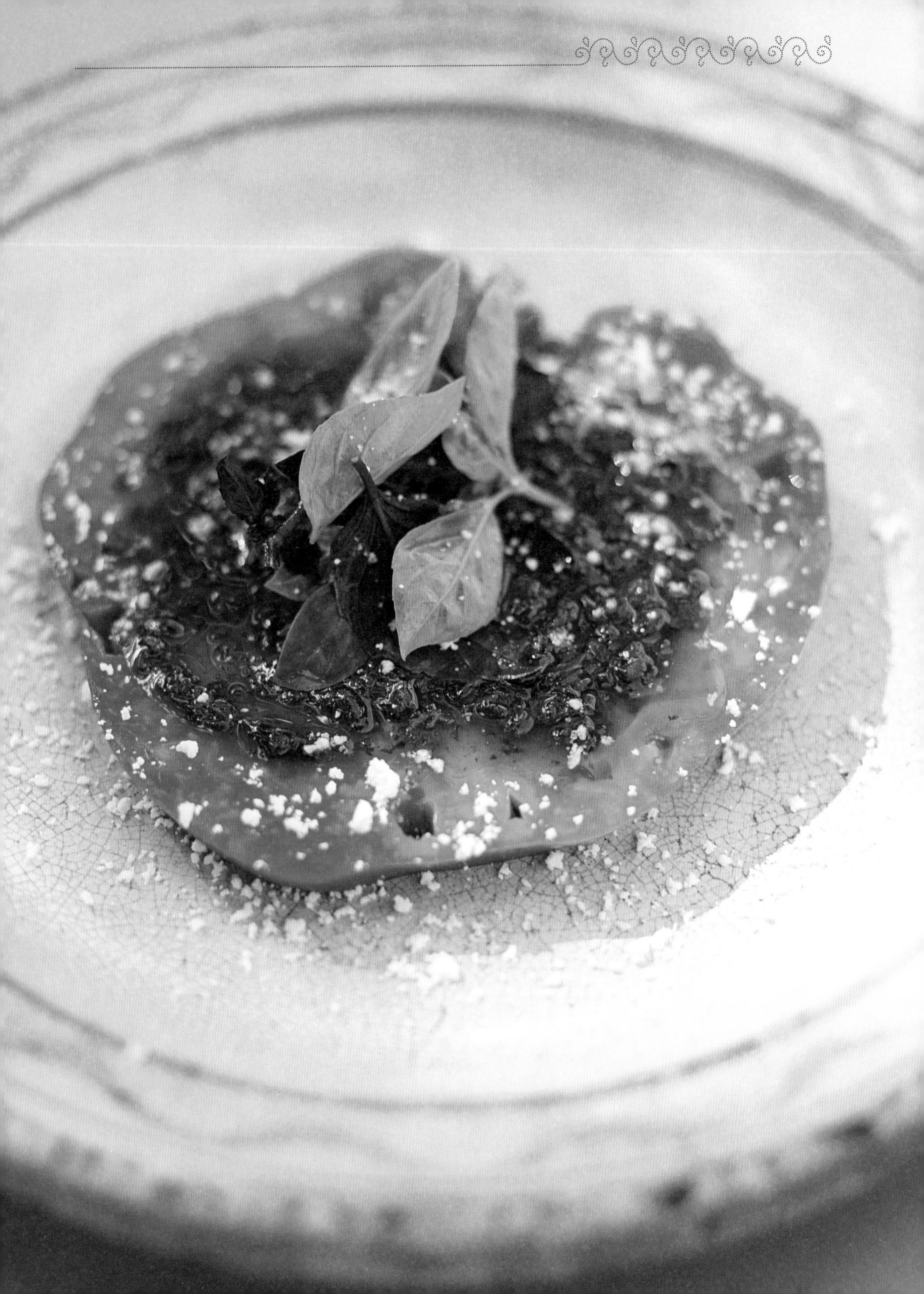

I've been in some funny places in my life looking for inspiration for cooking, but I never thought I'd find myself in a women's prison in the heart of Giudecca – a small inner island of Venice. These girls grow incredible vegetables and sell them outside the prison every Thursday. They sell out within the hour. It was my honor to be allowed in and to see a side of life I never thought I'd see. We put those great vegetables to use and cooked one of the most delicious minestrone soups I've ever tasted.

SPRING AND SUMMER MINESTRONE

- 3 cloves of garlic, peeled
- 7 ounces small carrots
- 7 ounces baby zucchini
- 1 large red onion, peeled
- 3 slices of bacon, the best quality you can afford
- olive oil
- 1 large tomato
- a bunch of fresh flat-leaf parsley
- 2 big handfuls of seasonal leaves, such as chard, beet greens or green cabbage
- 2 big handfuls of fresh peas
- 2 quarts plus ⅔ cup vegetable stock, preferably organic
- heaping ⅔ cup baby farfalle or other tiny pasta
- sea salt and freshly ground black pepper
- 2 big handfuls of soft round lettuce leaves
- ½ a head of radicchio or endive
- optional: a few zucchini flowers, torn

For the pesto

- a large bunch of fresh basil
- 2 small cloves of garlic
- 4 tablespoons pine nuts
- 1½ ounces Parmesan cheese
- extra virgin olive oil

It was early summer when I visited Venice, so obviously the things I put in this much-loved Italian soup were heavily influenced by the season. If you're going to make minestrone around the same time of year I did, this particular recipe will be fantastic. If it's winter just use more root vegetables and cabbage to create a different, but equally delicious version. I was given a gnarly old chunk of prosciutto when I made this, which I used in my soup base to add flavor. I've put bacon in the ingredients here, but you could also use a ham hock or a sizeable piece of pancetta if you like. Making the pounded homemade pesto to add to the soup while it's hot and steaming is a great thing to do. It adds a punch and flavor that's just incredible.

Finely slice the garlic, carrots and zucchini. Finely chop the onion and bacon. Get a large pan over medium heat and, once hot, add a few good lugs of olive oil, the onion, garlic, carrots and bacon. Stir well and cook for 5 minutes, then add the zucchini and cook for 3 to 4 minutes, or until soft. If you're going to use a ham hock or other big piece of meat for flavor, add that now, too.

Roughly chop the tomato and parsley (stalks and all) and shred your greens, adding everything to the pan as you go. Add the peas, then pour in your stock, making sure everything is covered, and bring to the boil. Once boiling, stir in the mini pasta and a pinch of salt and pepper. Bring to the boil, then turn down the heat and leave to simmer for 10 minutes. Have a quick taste to check the seasoning.

While your soup is cooking, make the pesto. Pick the basil leaves and keep the smaller ones to the side. Peel the garlic cloves. Pound the larger basil leaves in a pestle and mortar with a pinch of salt until they're really bruised and smelling fantastic. Add the pine nuts and garlic cloves and continue pounding until you've got a paste. Finely grate in the Parmesan, then loosen the pesto with extra virgin olive oil and mix well. Have a taste and really think about the flavors – you want to get a balance between the basil, the cheese and the salty kick, so add a little more of anything you think it needs.

Just before the soup is ready, shred the lettuce and radicchio and stir into the soup along with the zucchini flowers, if you have them. Check your seasoning once more, then divide the soup between your bowls, top with a really good dollop of pesto and drizzle over a little extra virgin olive oil. Finish by scattering over the smaller basil leaves.

FRIED SALAMI

Serves 4

- olive oil
- 12 large slices of salami (or 16 smaller ones)
- 1 sprig of fresh rosemary, leaves picked
- 2 cloves of garlic, peeled and finely sliced
- inside leaves from 1 radicchio, washed and spun dry
- good-quality balsamic vinegar
- sea salt and freshly ground black pepper
- Parmesan cheese

This is a delicious little starter or antipasto. There's something special about taking good-quality salami, slicing it a little thicker than usual, then frying it until just crisp. If you use the delicious juices left behind to quickly wilt radicchio, rosemary, garlic and balsamic together, you'll have an absolutely heavenly flavor combination. If you want to turn it into a snack to be reckoned with, you could tear a ball of buffalo mozzarella over crostini and use that as a base for this. These flavors and ingredients would also be amazing on top of a pizza, with a little taleggio and mozzarella. So next time you want to make an unusual but delicious starter that is Italy personified, go for this.

Drizzle a good lug of olive oil into a large frying pan and place over medium heat. Once hot, add the salami to the pan and fry for a couple of minutes, turning occasionally, until crispy. You might need to do this in batches so you don't overcrowd the pan. Transfer to a plate.

Once you've fried all the salami, leave the pan on the heat and add the rosemary leaves and garlic. Fry for a minute, then toss in the radicchio leaves. Let them wilt down gently, then add a good drizzle of balsamic vinegar, return the salami to the pan and toss again.

Take the pan off the heat and have a taste, seasoning with salt and pepper if needed. Put a few slices of fried salami on each plate and top with your warm salad and a few shavings of Parmesan. Drizzle over any juices left in the pan, then serve with toasted bread and tuck in.

BEEF STEAK VENETIAN STYLE

Serves 4

- 2 pound rib-eye steak, on the bone
- 4 sprigs of fresh rosemary
- sea salt and freshly ground black pepper
- extra virgin olive oil
- 3 tablespoons butter
- 1 clove of garlic, peeled and halved

For the salsa

- 1 fresh red chile
- 8 cherry tomatoes
- 1 clove of garlic, peeled
- a small bunch of fresh flat-leaf parsley
- a small bunch of fresh basil
- 1 tablespoon balsamic vinegar
- 3 tablespoons extra virgin olive oil
- 1½ ounces salted ricotta or feta cheese

This is a classic dish of Italy and I'm serving it with a great little salsa, which will really get the flavors rocking and rolling together. It's the perfect meal for meat-lovers, as the steak is the star of the show here. One thing I will say is that it's really important to use your instincts when cooking a beautiful piece of meat like this. I'm giving you some general guidelines here, but if you want a bit more guidance go to www.jamieoliver.com/how-to and watch the video to see what cooking the perfect steak is all about.

Take the meat out of the fridge. If one end is thicker than the other, pat it down until roughly the same thickness all over, and put it into a bowl with the finely chopped leaves from 2 rosemary sprigs. Add a few good pinches of pepper and a lug of extra virgin olive oil. Toss and flip the steak over until well coated, then rub the flavors into the meat. Cover with plastic wrap and leave to one side for an hour to soak up the flavors and come to room temperature. If you want the flavors to be really intense, cover and pop in the fridge for 5 to 6 hours. Take out 30 minutes before cooking.

Meanwhile, put a grill pan over high heat or get your grill lit and let it get really hot. Prick the chile all over with a sharp knife. Put your tomatoes and chile on the hot pan and cook until charred and blistered on all sides. Once ready, put them into a bowl and cover with plastic wrap. Once cool, peel off most of their skins. Halve the chile lengthways and get rid of the seeds. Preheat your oven to 400°F.

Put an ovenproof pan over high heat and when the pan is screaming hot, add the steak. You're going to cook it for 4 minutes to give it some beautiful color, so turn it every minute. After 2 minutes add a knob of butter to the pan. Using your 2 remaining rosemary sprigs, brush the steak with melted butter as it cooks to add flavor. Add another knob of butter when you flip it for the last time, then take the pan off the heat. Carefully pour away the fat, then put the pan straight in the hot oven to cook.

As a general guideline, cooking the steak for 10 to 12 minutes will give you rare meat, 15 to 17 minutes will give you rare to medium rare, and around 20 to 22 minutes will give you medium. Really it's up to you to pay attention and use your instincts. However you decide to cook it, turn it halfway through the cooking time. Once cooked to your liking, transfer to a plate for 5 minutes to rest. Rub the meat with the cut side of the garlic. Put a knob of butter or a drizzle of extra virgin olive oil on top.

While the meat rests, chop and finely slice the tomatoes, chile, garlic and herbs on a board. Put everything into a bowl and add the balsamic vinegar and extra virgin olive oil. Crumble in the cheese, mix around, and add a pinch of salt and pepper. Check the flavors, adding more seasoning or vinegar if needed. Carve the meat into slices, get rid of any fat, then sprinkle over some salt. Drizzle any resting juices from the plate into the salsa and over the steak for extra flavor, then serve with a nice salad.

WHITE POLENTA WITH BEEF INVOLTINI

Serves 4

- 8 x 3½ ounce minute or cube steaks
- sea salt and freshly ground black pepper
- heaping ⅔ cup freshly grated Parmesan cheese
- 4 sprigs of fresh rosemary, leaves picked and finely chopped
- 2 large cloves of garlic, peeled and finely chopped
- olive oil
- 1 onion, peeled and very finely chopped
- 1 celery stalk, trimmed and very finely chopped
- 1 teaspoon fennel seeds, bashed up
- ½ a fresh red chile, deseeded and finely chopped
- 1¼ cups red wine
- a few sprigs of fresh flat-leaf parsley, roughly chopped
- a large handful of mushrooms, such as chanterelles or any other nice eating mushrooms, brushed clean
- 1 28 ounce can of chopped tomatoes
- heaping ¾ cup white polenta
- a good knob of butter

Delizioso! Involtini is a classic way of taking a cheap cut of beef and cooking it in a way that makes it melt-in-the-mouth and delicious. If you ask your butcher for minute or cube steaks, he'll know to bash them out and will save you a step of preparation! Essentially this is a basic tomato and wine-based stew, to which you add various seasonal ingredients for nuances of flavor. You'll get incredible depth from the red wine, beef and wild mushrooms, and a nice sweetness from the tomatoes. Next to or on top of a spoonful of delicious polenta it's a winner, so go for it.

Lay the slices of beef on a chopping board between 2 pieces of plastic wrap and bash them with a heavy-based pan or rolling pin to flatten them out to about ¼ inch thick and the size of a postcard. Season with salt and pepper, and sprinkle over enough grated Parmesan to cover the surface of each steak. Scatter over half the chopped rosemary and all the chopped garlic. Roll each slice up tightly and secure well with cocktail sticks or the stripped sprigs of rosemary.

Heat a few good lugs of olive oil in a large pan over a very high heat. Add the rolled-up steaks and brown on all sides – this will take about 5 minutes. Once browned, remove to a plate and pour away the fat from the pan. Add a fresh lug of olive oil to the pan and add the onion, celery, fennel seeds and chile. Fry for 5 minutes, stirring as you go, until the onions have softened.

Return the steaks to the pan and pour in the red wine. Add the chopped parsley with the rest of the rosemary and the mushrooms and continue to cook until the liquid has reduced by half. Add the canned tomatoes and just cover with water. Bring to the boil, season lightly with salt and add a good pinch of pepper, then lower the heat and cover the pan with a lid, leaving it slightly askew. Cook for 1½ to 2 hours, or until the meat is tender, stirring from time to time and adding a splash of water if the sauce looks too thick. When it's perfectly cooked, have a taste and season to perfection.

About 40 minutes before your involtini are due to be ready, put 3½ cups of water on to boil with 1 teaspoon of sea salt. Once boiling, whisk in the polenta in a steady stream. Stir for 1 minute, and turn the heat down to low when it starts to bubble and spit. Put a lid on and leave to cook, stirring occasionally. You want it to be the consistency of oozy oatmeal, so keep an eye on it and add a splash of water if it looks too thick. After 40 minutes, remove from the heat and beat in most of the remaining Parmesan and the butter. Season to taste with salt and pepper.

Transfer the polenta to a large platter, or divide between your serving plates. Spoon over the gorgeous involtini with its fantastic sauce, scatter over your last little bit of Parmesan and serve immediately (but remind your guests to watch out for those little cocktail sticks).

Venice is a city on stilts in the middle of the Adriatic, so as you can imagine, its markets are full of incredible fish and seafood. They get stuff from all around the Mediterranean as well. It's a fish lover's paradise.

VENETIAN FISH STEW

Serves 4-6

- 6 large ripe beefsteak tomatoes, or 1 28 ounce can of chopped tomatoes
- 10½ ounces clams
- approximately 10 ½ ounces small squid tubes, with tentacles and wings, cleaned
- olive oil
- 1 red onion, peeled and sliced
- 2 cloves of garlic, peeled and finely sliced
- 3 anchovy fillets
- ½ teaspoon fennel seeds
- 5 or 6 black or green olives, pitted and squashed
- 2 fresh bay leaves
- 4 tiger shrimp
- 1 small sea bass, fins removed, scaled, gutted, cleaned and cut in half
- 1 medium rouget, fins removed, scaled, gutted, cleaned and cut in half
- ⅔ cup prosecco or white wine
- sea salt and freshly ground black pepper
- juice of ½ a lemon, plus 1 lemon, cut into wedges, to serve
- 1¼ cups hot vegetable or chicken stock, preferably organic
- 1 loaf of ciabatta, sliced
- extra virgin olive oil
- a few sprigs of fresh flat-leaf parsley, leaves picked
- optional: a handful of zucchini flowers

Fish stew like this is something everyone should experience. It's not one of those pretty stews, where you have delicate fillets of fish; this is proper rustic. If you don't want to include the more expensive stuff like tiger shrimp, that's OK. Use whatever cheaper fresh fish you like, just make sure it's caught sustainably and is nice and fresh (see introduction). I used a glass of prosecco because everyone in Venice drinks it and it was great value, but again, swapping that for whatever white wine you like would be no bad thing. Just follow the general idea of this recipe and you'll have something incredible. Dip your bread in it, slurp it up, get your fingers in there ... just enjoy it!

Cut a small cross in the top and bottom of your beefsteak tomatoes. Drop them into a pan of boiling water and leave them for around 30 seconds or so, until the skin starts to come away. Plunge them into cold water, then, once cool enough to handle, peel, deseed and finely chop them. If you're making this in winter months feel free to use canned tomatoes instead.

Give your clams a good scrub in plenty of water. If there are any that aren't tightly closed, give them a tap. If they don't close, throw them away. Lay the squid flat on your chopping board and insert a chopping knife inside the squid to protect the bottom as you use another knife to score along the top (as in the picture). This is about aesthetics, but it also helps the squid to cook beautifully and cling on to the sauce. Put to one side.

Put a large, wide saucepan over very high heat and add a good lug of olive oil. Add the onion, garlic, anchovies, fennel seeds, squashed olives and bay leaves. Fry fast for 3 or 4 minutes and keep it all moving around. Add the shrimp, clams, sea bass, rouget, squid, prosecco and chopped or canned tomatoes. Add a good pinch of salt and pepper, then put the lid on and turn down to low heat so it's just simmering away. After 12 minutes, have a taste, and at this point add the lemon juice, seasoning if needed, and enough stock to get it to the consistency you like. By now, the clams should have opened and the fish should be cooked. Turn the heat down really low.

Get a grill pan on high heat and toast your ciabatta slices until lovely and charred. Drizzle with a little extra virgin olive oil. If there are any closed clams, pick them out of the stew and throw them away. Scatter the parsley leaves and torn zucchini flowers, if you have them, over the stew and drizzle over a good lug of extra virgin olive oil. Serve with lemon wedges on the side for squeezing over.

Cooking with my fishermen mates was really good fun. Eating good seafood and good pasta is normal for these guys, so I wanted to feed them something really delicious. This vongole is fast and tasty, so it was perfect. We had a good laugh over a bottle of prosecco at the fact that we weren't the only ones getting fed. The mosquitoes were having a field day!

SPAGHETTI VONGOLE

Serves 4

- 2 pounds small clams, scrubbed clean (sustainably caught – see introduction)
- a small bunch of fresh flat-leaf parsley
- 4 cloves of garlic
- 10 cherry tomatoes
- 1 generous cup white wine
- 14 ounces dried spaghetti
- sea salt and freshly ground black pepper
- extra virgin olive oil
- 1-2 dried chiles

Clams were, and still are, available in Venice by the boatload. So much so that they're even considered peasant food. Although this recipe originates from Venice, it's so delicious that it's now become a classic Italian dish. People can be picky about whether or not it should be made with or without tomatoes, but personally I like the subtle color and sweetness they add to the dish. The most important thing about it is timing everything so you get perfectly steamed clams and al dente pasta. Once you've made it a couple of times your intuition will kick in and you'll be able to make it quickly and perfectly every time.

Put a pan of water on to boil. While that's happening, sort through your cleaned clams and if there are any that aren't tightly closed, give them a sharp tap. If they don't close, throw them away. Put a large pan with a lid over high heat and let it heat up. Finely slice the parsley stalks, then put them to one side and roughly chop the leaves. Peel and chop the garlic, quarter the tomatoes and get your wine ready.

Add the pasta to the boiling water with a good pinch of salt and cook according to packet instructions until al dente. About 5 minutes before your pasta is ready, get ready to start cooking - you'll have to be quick about this, so no mucking about! Put 4 generous lugs of extra virgin olive oil into the hot pan and add the garlic, parsley stalks and a good pinch of salt and pepper. Crumble in the dried chile and add the chopped tomatoes. Stir everything around constantly and just as the garlic starts to color, tip in the clams and pour in the wine. It will splutter and steam, so give everything a good shake and put the lid on the pan. After about 3 or 4 minutes the clams will start to open, so keep shuffling the pan around until all of them have opened. Take the pan off the heat. Get rid of any clams that haven't opened.

By now your pasta should be just about perfect. Drain and add to the pan of clams along with the parsley leaves and an extra drizzle of extra virgin olive oil. Stir or toss for a further minute or two to let the beautiful seashore juices from the clams be absorbed into the pasta. Serve right away. No sane Italian would eat this dish without some fresh hunks of bread to mop up the juices. Beautiful!

P.S. The first time you make this it will be good, but you might find things don't come together exactly at the right time. But don't worry, this dish is all about confidence and the more you make this, the more you'll find the pasta and clams are ready and perfect at the same time. And then it will be great!

Italy has great wine bars, not to mention countless shops selling pastries, gelato and lovely little cookies of every description. There's no way you can visit Venice without enjoying a glass (or bottle!) of prosecco. The city's famous Bellini – a mixture of peach and prosecco – is my mum's idea of heaven!

NINI BELLINI

Serves 6

- 2 ripe peaches, flat ones if you can get them
- 1 bottle of chilled prosecco

I've named this beautiful cocktail after Leo Caplan's wife, Janine (or "Nini" as she's known by her nearest and dearest). Leo made a really generous donation to a charity called Help a London Child, and in return I said I'd name a recipe in this book after his lovely wife!

A peach Bellini is the classic Venetian cocktail, and my mate Arrigo serves loads of them in his world-famous establishment, Harry's Bar. Arrigo's granddad, Giuseppe Cipriani, opened Harry's in 1931, and because he was a bit of a genius he ended up inventing not only this beautiful cocktail but also another thing I absolutely love – carpaccio. The story goes that when Giuseppe first made this cocktail the sun was setting and the colors in the drink were the same as the colors in his favorite Bellini painting ... you can work out the rest! You can also get nice results using canned peaches if you can't find beautifully ripe flat peaches.

I think this is best made just before serving, in front of your friends. Halve your peaches, remove their stones, then pop them into a blender and blitz until smooth. Add a splash of water if needed and put the purée into a jug. If you don't have a blender just use your hands to squeeze, mash and really push the peaches through a sieve so you get as much as possible of their wonderful flavor and the color from their skins into the purée. You can get the purée as fine as you like, but I don't mind the thickness ... it's quite rustic. Discard (or eat!) whatever is left behind in the sieve, then pour your prosecco into the jug and gently mix together. Divide between six glasses right away, and top up with a little more prosecco if need be, and enjoy!

P.S. The spirit of the Bellini isn't exclusive to peaches – nectarines or berries are also lovely used in the same way. There could easily be a Bellini for every month of the year.

BEST TIRAMISÙ

Serves 12

- 9 ounces good-quality dark chocolate (70% cocoa solids)
- 3 tablespoons butter, diced
- sea salt
- 6 or 7 ounces ladyfingers
- 1¾ cups good hot sweetened coffee
- Vin Santo or other sweet dessert wine like Marsala
- 4 large eggs, preferably free-range or organic
- ⅓ cup plus 1 tablespoon sugar
- 1½ pounds mascarpone
- 2 oranges
- a few fresh coffee beans, bashed up finely

For me (and Italians would kill me for saying this), tiramisù is the coolest trifle in the world. The Venetians don't really have many desserts, but this is a classic. It's usually dead simple and all about the ladyfingers, the coffee and the cream, but I think chocolate and coffee are such good friends that you've got to get a bit of chocolate in there. I've also used egg whites, which isn't traditional, but they make it lovely and light and spread the mascarpone about so it's not so rich.

Put a glass bowl over a pan of gently simmering water, making sure the water doesn't touch the base of the bowl. Put 7 ounces of the chocolate into the bowl, keeping the rest in one piece. Add the diced butter and a pinch of salt, and leave for 5 minutes or so until melted and combined. Help it along by giving it a stir every now and then.

Meanwhile, line a large, deep bowl or round earthenware dish (about 12 inches in diameter and 4½ inches deep) with the laldyfingers, then carefully pour over the hot sweetened coffee. Add a couple of swigs of Vin Santo to your melted chocolate, stir it through, then drizzle all over the ladyfingers. Use a spatula to carefully smooth it out to the edges so you've got a nice even layer. Put it to one side to cool.

Separate your eggs, putting the whites into one bowl and the yolks into another. Add the sugar to the yolks with another swig of Vin Santo (if you're feeling naughty!), and beat with an electric mixer on the highest setting for about 5 minutes, or by hand, until all the sugar has dissolved and the yolks are pale and fluffy. Mix in the mascarpone and the zest of 1 orange.

Clean and dry your beaters, and, in another bowl, beat the whites with a pinch of salt until they form stiff peaks – they should be a similar consistency to the yolk and mascarpone mixture, and should hold their shape when you lift the beaters from the bowl.

Using a large metal spoon, add a spoonful of your whites to the yolk mixture and gently fold them in, then fold through the rest of the whites. Spoon and smooth this creamy mixture on top of your chocolate layer.

Scatter the finely bashed-up coffee beans over the top. Using a sharp knife or a peeler, carefully shave over your remaining chocolate. Finely grate over the zest from half your remaining orange. Pop the tiramisù into the fridge for 2 hours to set.

ACCIUGAE SALATE
€ 19,00
371 SICILIA

SPIDER CRABS *Granceola* is the Italian name for large **spider crabs** with a delicate sweet meat. After boiling, the meat is cleaned, picked and served simply in the shell with oil, fresh parsley and lemon juice, or stirred through pasta and risottos.

BABY CLAMS *Caparozzolo* is the Venetian name for *vongole* or **baby clams** - a great variety of them can be found around the Venetian lagoons. They are usually eaten with spaghetti, in risotto or simply with a squeeze of lemon juice.

POLENTA AND PARMESAN **Polenta** is dried white or yellow corn that is ground to a fine grain, then stirred into boiling water until thick and creamy. Delicious with grated **Parmesan** cheese beaten in.

ASPARAGUS Beautiful green and white **asparagus** grows all around the Veneto region, and is added to everything from risottos to pasta or simply grilled until tender.

PROSECCO AND GRAPPA

Prosecco is a dry sparkling wine and the aperitif of choice in Venice, mixed with peach purée for the famous Bellini. **Grappa**, a clear strong spirit, is often served as a *digestivo* or after-dinner drink.

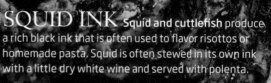

SQUID INK

Squid and cuttlefish produce a rich black ink that is often used to flavor risottos or homemade pasta. Squid is often stewed in its own ink with a little dry white wine and served with polenta.

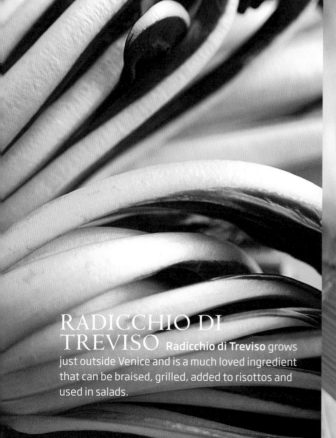

RADICCHIO DI TREVISO

Radicchio di Treviso grows just outside Venice and is a much loved ingredient that can be braised, grilled, added to risottos and used in salads.

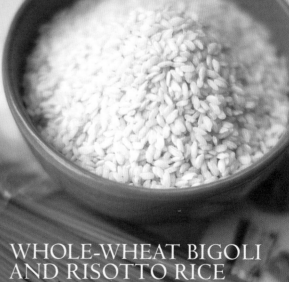

WHOLE-WHEAT BIGOLI AND RISOTTO RICE

Bigoli is whole-wheat spaghetti, and **risotto rice** forms the basis of the creamy, starchy risotto dishes so famous in the north of Italy.

SWEDEN

SWEDEN

Cities like London, Paris and Rome get talked about a lot, and yes, they are big wonderful cities, but there are equally brilliant "must-go" places that fly slightly under the radar. Stockholm is one of them.

Not only is it a beautiful city to look at, it is also clean, really organized, funky and stylish. The people are gorgeous and really know how to enjoy life. With its great food markets, fairs, shops, restaurants and waterfront you'll never be short of things to do in Stockholm.

The city is made up of fourteen main islands, so there are bridges and waterways everywhere, which is why it is often called "the Venice of the North." The old town, Gamla Stan, is one of the most beautiful medieval cities around. I spent a morning poking my head into some of its wonderful little shops and bakeries, sitting in the square and drinking hot chocolate with the locals, and I couldn't have been happier.

One of the big bonuses of being in a city surrounded by this much water is that you're never far away from fresh fish and seafood. Sweden's strict environmental laws mean the clean, cold water in Stockholm's river Norrström is home to a plethora of great fish, which can be caught in the internal rivers of the city. These fish have grown more slowly and developed denser meat than fish from warmer waters. Since the 1980s, Sweden has had fairly relaxed fishing laws, so it's not uncommon at all to see people fishing along the waterfront or sailing off to catch pike, perch, Baltic herring and pikeperch for their dinner – what a beautiful thing to be able to do in your own city.

Stockholm big enough to be interesting, yet small enough to feel welcoming and friendly. And the people are real characters, but sane (which is something you can really appreciate when you live in a city like London!). In general, this is one of the most accessible cities to visit if you're looking for an easy, chilled-out couple of days. I don't want to sound too lazy, but everyone I met, from the bloke selling reindeer meat at the market stall to the kids fishing at the waterfront, spoke ridiculously good English and even had nicer English accents than me! I think sometimes when you travel it's good to know you can experience a completely different culture but still have the option of talking to the locals, asking them questions and finding out what's going on around you.

Most people don't realize Swedish food is a force to be reckoned with, but it absolutely is, and I hope the recipes in this chapter convince you of that. I was blown away by the clean, refined flavors I found. Their long, harsh winters have made the Swedes some of the best preservers in the world, and that comes through in their hero ingredients and dishes, from the delicate flavors of gravlax, to their mind-blowing array of pickles and their delicious smoked meats.

Without question, Swedish food has benefited from the country's historical involvement in the spice trade. They've managed to combine those faraway flavors with their own local ingredients in really interesting ways. Whether it's the subtle hint of caraway seeds in a soft pastry or a recklessly bold, but brilliant, use of cumin with fish, they don't mess around. I found massive surprises in the cooking I saw there ... And that's what this book is all about.

Another big surprise was finding out that the Swedes are one of the biggest coffee consumers in the world, second only to (wait for it, another surprise) ... Finland! So as you can imagine, coffee culture is a big thing and Stockholm is full of coffee shops selling beautiful pastries and breads. Some are elegant, soft and relatively French in style; others are knotty sourdough buns loaded with pungent spices like cloves and cardamom and finished with sugar. Just goes to show that when you use flavors with real confidence, things you wouldn't think would work, really do.

I expected the other five countries I visited for this book to show me exciting stuff, and although I knew Sweden would be great I didn't expect it to make my eyes pop out of my head in the same way. But it turns out that Swedish food was the underdog that kicked ass in this book! I ate wonderful food, visited islands in the archipelago, spent time in the great outdoors and soaked up as much Swedish culture (and schnapps, or "snaps" as the locals call it!) as I could. But perhaps the most interesting thing about the whole trip was that despite all the running around I did, I came back feeling fresh, re-energized and totally up for the week ahead. On some level, I think the food probably had something to do with that. Hopefully the recipes in this chapter will help reinforce something I now know: Swedish food is big, bold, brave and definitely up there with the best in the world.

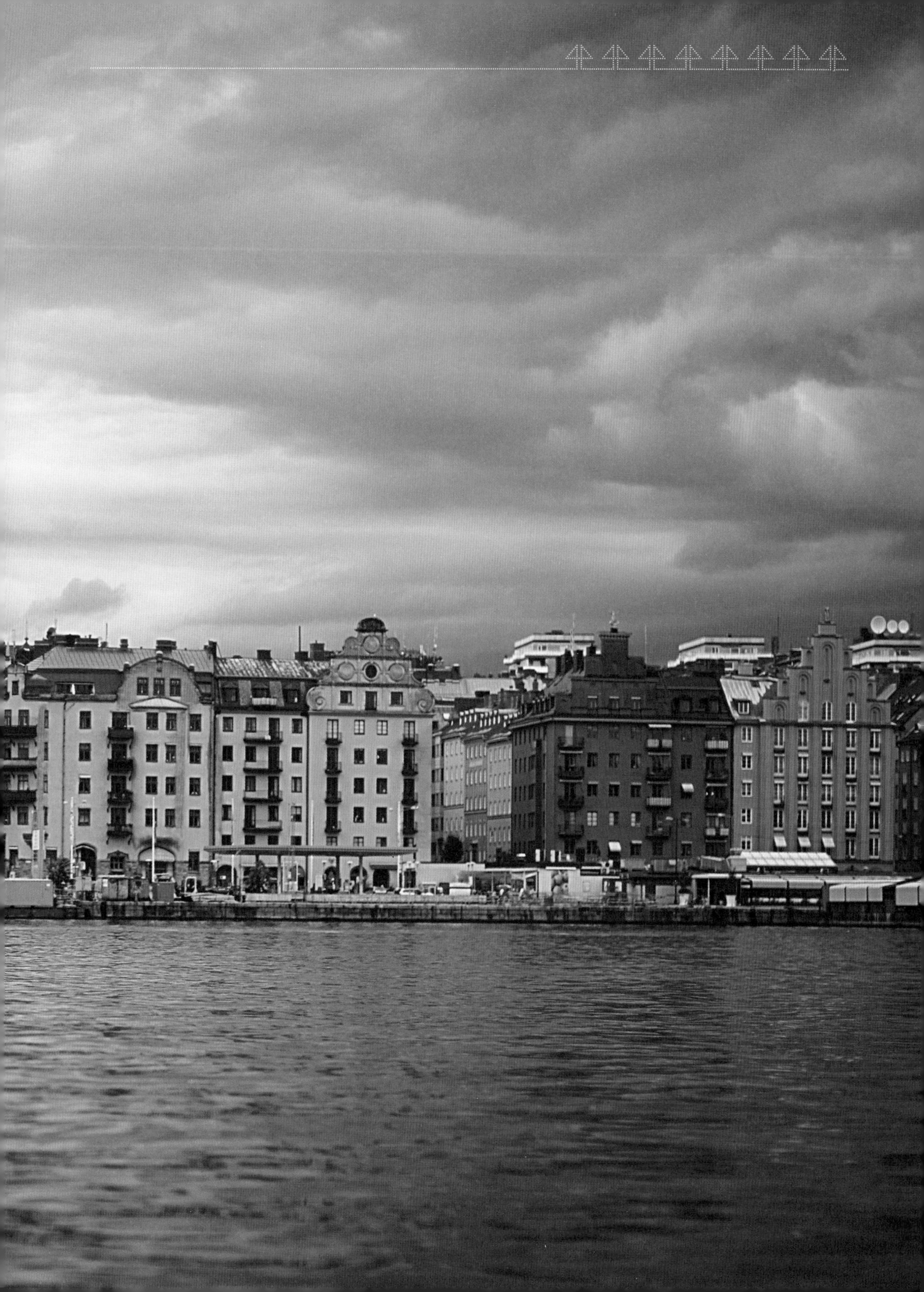

SWEDISH MEATBALLS

Serves 4-6

For the meatballs

- a handful of mixed fresh herbs, such as dill, flat-leaf parsley or chives, roughly chopped
- 10½ ounces ground pork, the best quality you can afford
- 10½ ounces ground beef
- 1 large egg, preferably free-range or organic
- a scant ½ cup milk
- ¼ cup dried breadcrumbs
- 1 teaspoon ground allspice
- sea salt and freshly ground black pepper
- olive oil

For the sauce

- juice of ½ a lemon
- 1¼ cups beef stock, preferably organic (if using a bouillon cube, ½ is enough)
- 1 tablespoon all-purpose flour
- ¼ cup heavy cream
- 7 ounces of lingonberry, cranberry, blackberry or blackcurrant jam, to serve

Even people who don't know much about Swedish food will probably at least have heard of, or tried, the great dish that is Swedish meatballs - especially since Ikea took over the world (I've been told they sell loads of these in their cafeterias). Paired with mashed potato and warm lingonberry sauce, they make a perfect meal: tasty, comforting, with a hint of sweetness. If you've got a load of people coming for dinner you could make a batch or two of these and let everyone help themselves.

These meatballs are easy to make; just make sure you've got a wide casserole-type pan. It will make your life easier and you'll use it all the time, so it's worth investing in.

Set aside a few of the herbs, then put the rest into a large bowl with the pork, beef, egg, milk, breadcrumbs and allspice. Add a good pinch of salt and pepper, then get your clean hands in there and scrunch and mix it well. Divide the mixture in half, then pat and roll each half into a sausage shape. Cut each one into 15 equal pieces, then wet your hands and roll 30 little balls. Keep wetting your hands as you go so you get nice round elegant meatballs. Put them on a large oiled plate, then cover with plastic wrap and pop into the fridge for 1 hour to firm up.

When you're ready to cook, put your largest pan on a medium heat and add a lug of olive oil. Once hot, add the meatballs and fry gently for 10 to 15 minutes, tossing occasionally, until they are golden brown.

Transfer the meatballs to a large plate. Spoon away any excess fat from the pan, then add the lemon juice, a splash of stock, the flour, the cream, a heaped tablespoon of lingonberry or other jam and a good pinch of salt and pepper. Stir constantly, adding splashes of stock until you've used it all. Bring to the boil, then turn the heat down and reduce until you have a nice consistency that will cling to the meatballs. Taste it, then season with a pinch of salt and pepper. Return the meatballs to the pan and move them around so they get coated in the sauce.

Serve your meatballs - 8 per person is about right - drizzled with any lovely sauce left in the pan and with a few spoonfuls of warmed-up jam on top. They'll go brilliantly next to mashed or crispy potatoes, or even rice, but personally, I love these on top of smashed celeriac mash. Sprinkle over your reserved chopped herbs and tuck in!

SPLIT PEA SOUP

Serves 6

- olive oil
- 2 sticks of celery, trimmed and finely diced
- 2 onions, peeled and finely chopped
- ½ teaspoon dried thyme
- ½ teaspoon dried marjoram or oregano
- 1 pound dried yellow split peas, thoroughly washed
- 9 ounce piece of cooked, smoked ham, the best quality you can afford
- 6⅓ cups chicken stock, preferably organic
- sea salt and freshly ground black pepper
- extra virgin olive oil
- mustard of your choice, to serve
- crispbread, to serve

The Swedes have been tucking into this hearty pea soup since the Middle Ages. Back then, everyone would fill their bellies with this on a Thursday to get them ready for the Christian fast that started on Friday. As a nod to that tradition, Thursday is still "split pea soup" day in the army and the navy. I stopped by the Royal Guards' Barracks in Stockholm to meet some soldiers and taste this famous soup. It's very close in taste and texture to a dish we've been making in Britain for hundreds of years, pease pudding. Just proves that old saying: "If it ain't broke, don't fix it!" Like us, the Swedes often cook their yellow split peas with a joint of ham or bacon. If you're feeling a bit nostalgic and in need of some frumpy, comforting food this is a brilliant thing to make.

Get a large pan over low heat and add a good lug of olive oil. Once hot, add the celery, onions and dried herbs and cook for 10 minutes, stirring occasionally, until soft but not colored.

Add your washed peas and ham, pour in the stock and bring to the boil. Reduce to a gentle simmer over medium to low heat, then pop the lid on and cook for around 50 minutes, or until the peas are lovely and soft. Use tongs to pull out the ham and move it to a board. Chop and shred it up, discarding any rind and fatty pieces. Roughly mash the peas with a potato masher to give a nice texture, then stir in your shredded ham. Have a taste and season with salt and pepper.

Divide the soup between your bowls, drizzle with a little extra virgin olive oil, and serve with a good dollop of mustard on the side to pimp the flavor and some nice crispbread for dipping.

PIKEPERCH AND ROASTED BEET SALAD

Serves 4

- sea salt and freshly ground black pepper
- 1 lemon
- ⅔ cup sour cream
- 4 x 5 to 6 ounce fillets of pikeperch (or cod, halibut, haddock, sea bass), scaled and pinboned (sustainably caught – see introduction)
- olive oil
- 1 teaspoon caraway seeds
- 10½ ounces spinach leaves, washed and spun dry
- a few knobs of butter
- extra virgin olive oil

For the roasted beet salad

- kosher salt
- 1½ pounds of red, white and Chioggia beets, scrubbed clean
- a small bunch of fresh chives, finely sliced
- a small bunch of fresh dill, with flowers if you can get them, flowers reserved, leaves finely chopped
- 1 medium red onion, peeled and finely sliced
- red wine vinegar
- extra virgin olive oil

Freshwater pikeperch is local to Stockholm, but if you live elsewhere any other firm white fish, such as halibut, cod, haddock or sea bass, will be delicious in its place. This dish is all about showing off great fish by cooking it simply and teaming it with really exciting veg like these beets. As the beets roast on the tray of kosher salt they'll pick up a bit of seasoning but also get soft, sweet and delicious. Before this trip I would never have thought to put caraway seeds with fish or quite as many herbs in the salad (and I love my herbs), but the Swedes are so brave with their spices and herbs that I felt inspired to follow their bold approach.

Preheat your oven to 400°F. Scatter a few handfuls of kosher salt around the base of a baking sheet. Cut the bottom off each beet and stand them up on the salt. Pop into the oven to cook for 1 hour. Mix a little pinch of salt and a good squeeze of lemon juice into your sour cream and put to one side.

Once the beets are beautifully roasted, take them out of the oven and turn the temperature right down to its lowest setting. Let the beets cool down a little, then peel them and discard their skins. Quarter the darker purple beets and put to one side. Halve, quarter and slice the rest of the beets and put those into a bowl with the chives, most of the dill and the sliced onion. Add a pinch of salt and pepper, pour in a splash of red wine vinegar and a lug of extra virgin olive oil, and use your hands to toss everything together really well.

Put a large pan over medium to high heat. Pinch the skin side of each fish fillet and lightly score a few times, 1 inch apart. You just want shallow incisions. Rub some olive oil, salt and pepper all over each fillet. Lay them in the hot pan, skin side down, cook for about 3 minutes, until the skin is crispy, then flip them over and cook for 1 minute more, until cooked through.

Add the caraway seeds, reserved dill (if you have any dill flowers, add those too) and spinach leaves. Sprinkle over a pinch of salt and leave for about 30 to 60 seconds, until the spinach starts to wilt down. At that point, take the pan off the heat, dot a few knobs of butter over the spinach, and squeeze over the juice of ½ the lemon.

Quickly toss the reserved dark purple beets into the rest of your beet salad and divide between your plates. Top each salad with some of your spinach and a fillet of fish. The juices from the bottom of the pan are absolute gold, so spoon those over the fish too. Finish with a dollop of sour cream and a drizzle of extra virgin olive oil and serve right away.

Human jeopardy, stress and survival skills are often behind some of the world's most brilliant recipes. Burying and curing big sides of fish for gravlax was the Swedish solution to food shortages during their harsh winters. Adding beets and a little schnapps to their traditional recipe turns an already beautiful food into something really vibrant and dramatic.

GORGEOUS BEET GRAVLAX

Serves 10 as a starter

For the fish

- 1 side of salmon fillet, skin on and pinboned (approximately 1½ pounds) (sustainably caught – see introduction)
- ⅔ cup plus 1 tablespoon kosher salt
- 3 tablespoons demerara sugar
- 2½ tablespoons fresh horseradish, peeled and finely grated (or jarred grated horseradish)
- 10½ ounces raw beets, peeled and coarsely grated
- ¼ cup plain schnapps or vodka
- a large bunch of fresh dill, with flowers if you can get them, flowers reserved, leaves finely chopped
- 1 lemon

For the creamy sauce

- scant cup sour cream
- 1-2 heaped teaspoons whole grain mustard
- a good pinch of sea salt and freshly ground black pepper
- zest and juice of ½ a lemon
- a small handful of fresh dill, finely chopped

I've been making gravlax since I was ten years old, long before I knew it was Swedish. The word "gravlax" actually comes from the Scandinavian word for "grave," because historically they'd wrap their salmon fillets in beech bark and bury them with bricks on top to really help push the salt into the fish and cure it.

This beautiful and delicate dish sums up everything I love about Swedish food: it's elegant, clean and fresh, and not only does it look incredible, it's also a doddle to make. If you've got family or friends coming round, you'll be so proud of yourself when you wow them with the finished product. Of course you can buy it ready-made at the supermarket, but there's something so exciting and special about doing your own, so why not?

Place the salmon on a large baking sheet, skin side down, and spoon the kosher salt evenly all over the fish – this will draw the moisture out and make it dense and firm enough to carve. Scatter over the sugar to give some sweetness, then spread the grated horseradish and beets all over the salmon so that the flesh is completely covered. Gently pat it down with your hands (you might want to put on some rubber gloves to prevent your hands getting stained). Drizzle over the schnapps, then sprinkle over all your chopped dill and a few dill flowers if you have them.

Finely grate over the zest of your lemon, then cover the tray of salmon tightly with plastic wrap. Pop a weight on top to help pack everything down (2 bottles of mineral water, or another baking sheet and a few tin cans, usually do the trick), then put it into the fridge for 48 hours.

After 2 days unwrap the fish and hold the fillet down while you pour away the juices from the tray. Use your hands to push away all the toppings (this can be really messy, so again you might want to wear rubber gloves and push the toppings straight into a plastic bag). Wipe everything off, then pat the fillet dry with paper towel.

Skin side down, starting at the tail end, carefully cut under the fillet with a really long sharp knife, separating the skin from the fillet. With long rocking motions, angle the knife down slightly towards the skin and carve along the length of the fillet to remove the skin. Trim off any brown bits of fish from underneath, then flip it back over. If you need more guidance, go to www.jamieoliver.com/how-to and we'll show you how to do this. Slice what you need as thinly as you can and arrange on a board or plate for serving. Wrap the rest of the fillet in plastic wrap and it will stay happily in your fridge for 2 weeks.

Before serving, mix all your sauce ingredients together. Have a taste, add a bit more dill or lemon juice if you think it needs it, and serve the sauce in a bowl next to your gravlax. Beside the crunchy salad on the next page this will be beautiful!

SIMPLE CRUNCHY SALAD

Serves 4

- 1 cucumber
- 1 red onion, peeled
- 3 small carrots
- 1 bulb of fennel,
  outer leaves peeled back,
  quartered lengthways
- 6 small radishes, quartered
- 1 tablespoon white
  wine vinegar
- 1 heaped teaspoon sugar
- 3 tablespoons extra virgin
  olive oil
- a small bunch of fresh dill,
  with flowers if you can
  get them, flowers reserved,
  leaves roughly chopped
- a small bunch of fresh
  flat-leaf parsley,
  finely chopped
- sea salt

One of the things I love about a good crunchy salad is that you can simply change it according to where you live and what fresh ingredients are available to you. It's a mighty fine salad to enjoy with steak, next to gravlax or simply on its own. All I'll say is that if something is hard and crunchy it's your job to prep it in a way that makes it a pleasure to eat. Having a mixture of shapes and sizes in your salad is always sweet, so use your imagination to make a bunch of regular stuff look, and taste, sexy. Chop some ingredients, slice others, and use a peeler or mandoline to create texture - just make sure your onion is finely sliced and you'll have something really simple and exciting.

Chuck all your vegetables into a large salad bowl as you prep them and you'll have this beautiful salad ready in no time at all. Halve your cucumber lengthways and use a teaspoon to get rid of the seeds. Finely slice each half. Finely slice the peeled onion. Use a peeler to peel your carrots into ribbons. Finely slice the fennel quarters. Add the radish quarters to the rest of the veg, then add the vinegar, sugar, extra virgin olive oil, dill and parsley to the bowl. Season with a good pinch of salt, then toss and scrunch everything together. Have a quick taste and adjust the seasoning, then sprinkle over the dill flowers, if you have them, to really make it zing and serve right away, while everything is full of flavor and crunch. Simple!

P.S. If you've got a food processor with a julienne slicer, or a coarse grater, you could simply use that to prep all the vegetables. It will look slightly more uniform, but if you've got it, you may as well use it!

SWEDISH CHICKEN CAESAR SALAD

Serves 4

- 2 teaspoons fennel seeds
- sea salt and freshly ground black pepper
- olive oil
- 4 x 5 to 6 ounce boneless chicken breasts, skin on, preferably free-range or organic
- 12 quail's eggs
- 7 ounces Swedish rye bread or regular rye bread
- 6 slices of bacon, the best quality you can afford
- 4 large handfuls of mixed interesting salad leaves such as mini red, little gem, radicchio, or red chicory, washed, spun dry and leaves roughly torn
- 1 small box of cress, snipped
- extra virgin olive oil
- Västerbotten, Parmesan or pecorino cheese, to serve

For the dressing
- 6 tablespoons sour cream
- juice of ½ a lemon
- a splash of white wine vinegar
- 4 anchovy fillets
- a small bunch of fresh dill

This is something I made up on my last day in Sweden. I thought playing around with the idea of a Caesar salad by swapping in a few key ingredients from the country would be a cool thing to do. So I used chunks of rye bread for my croutons, dill for some added flavor, a hard cheese called Västerbotten for shaving over, and fennel seeds to give the chicken a Swedish spirit. It tastes delicious and looks really beautiful on a massive platter in the middle of the table. If you have some leftover roasted chicken you want to use up, this is a great way of doing that.

Preheat your oven to 375°F. Gently bash the fennel seeds in a pestle and mortar with a good pinch of salt and pepper. Drizzle olive oil all over the chicken, then rub the fennel seed mixture all over them. Place on a baking sheet and put into the hot oven to bake for around 20 minutes, or until perfectly cooked through. Once cooked, leave the chicken on a plate to cool but keep the cooking juices to one side. Turn your oven up to 400°F.

While the chicken cooks, boil the quail's eggs for 2½ minutes, then remove with a slotted spoon and plunge them into a bowl of cold water. Drain, then carefully peel off their shells and put to one side.

Tear the rye bread into bite-sized chunks and toss these in the juices from the baking sheet, really rubbing them into the goodness so that they soak it up. When they are nicely coated, spread them around the sheet and lay the strips of bacon over them. Put the sheet back into the oven for around 10 minutes, until the bacon is golden, crispy and delicious, then take the sheet out and move everything to some paper towels to drain.

Put the sour cream, lemon, white wine vinegar, anchovies and a good pinch of salt and pepper into a blender and whiz until smooth. Have a taste to check the flavor—make sure it's a tiny bit too salty and acidic. Finely chop half your bunch of dill and stir this in, with a splash of water to make a clingy, but light dressing. Roughly tear your remaining dill into a large bowl and add your salad leaves.

Get rid of the chicken skin, then shred or pull the meat apart and add it to the bowl of salad leaves. Add your croutons and break in your pieces of bacon. Drizzle over the dressing and use your hands to quickly but delicately toss and dress everything. Place on a nice big platter, sprinkle over some cress, then halve your quail's eggs and arrange on top. Finish with a drizzle of extra virgin olive oil and some shavings of cheese, and take it right to the table so everyone can dig in.

"Surströmming" is the world-famous stinky herring. And boy, does it stink! But it's incredibly good for you and when it's lovingly put together on some crisp Swedish bread, with butter, a few slices of boiled potatoes, chopped red onion, tomato, dill and sour cream, all I can say is, it's delicious. Love it or hate it, you won't forget it!

PICKLED HERRING

Serves 4

- 4 large (approximately 3 ounces each) or 8 small pickled herring (sustainably caught – see introduction)
- 1 x 5 ounce container of sour cream
- a bunch of fresh chives, finely chopped
- 1 small red onion, peeled and very finely chopped
- optional: fish roe
- 1 lemon
- optional: dill flowers, to serve
- optional: rye bread and butter, to serve

Herring might be an underrated fish elsewhere in the world, but if I've learned anything on this trip it's that the Swedes take them incredibly seriously. They go to work pickling and preserving their herring in November, because by this time the fish have finished spawning and the texture of their flesh is dense and delicious again.

I'm so glad I became reacquainted with the joys of herring during my visit because I discovered really creative, mind-blowing flavors for pickling: everything from dill to red onion, cloves and even a curried mayo! Good supermarkets here should stock pickled herring, as will good fishmongers if you give them a few days' notice. You can also get them really easily from mail order/online sources like www.totallyswedish.com. They will sit happily in your fridge, begging to be used as a fabulous starter, or as a main course with new potatoes and a simple green salad. I urge you to give them a try.

Lay 1 or 2 herring in the middle of each plate and spoon a few dollops of sour cream over each one. Top with a big handful of chopped chives and finely chopped onion, and a small spoonful of fish roe, if using. Finely grate some lemon zest over each portion, and garnish with some dill flowers if you have them. Serve next to some buttered slices of rye bread, with a wedge of lemon for squeezing over.

ARCTIC CHAR PARCELS

Serves 4

- 1 pound new potatoes
- sea salt and freshly ground black pepper
- 10½ ounces Swiss chard or spinach, washed and spun dry
- a small bunch of fresh dill, roughly chopped
- olive oil
- 4 x 7 ounce fillets of Arctic char, sea trout or salmon, skin on, scaled and pinboned (sustainably caught – see introduction)
- white wine vinegar
- a small bunch of fresh chives
- ½ cup sour cream, to serve

Please try Arctic char if you visit Sweden. It looks like a cross between a trout and a salmon and it loves the cold clean northern waters. Cold water tends to make things grow slowly, and quite often that means better flavor. This dish is slightly contradictory, because although it uses Swedish ingredients, the method isn't traditional. Swedes seem to like their plates to be quite deconstructed, so the different elements sit next to each other, but I think steaming everything in one parcel and cooking them together is a great thing to do. You can swap the elements here for whatever fish, veg and herbs you please, but the heart of the dish will be the same.

Preheat your oven to 350°F. Put the new potatoes into a pan of salted water, bring to the boil, then turn down the heat and simmer for 10 to 15 minutes, until just cooked. Drain and put them back into the pan to steam dry.

Meanwhile, if using chard, finely slice the stems on an angle, then roll the leaves into a sort of cigar shape and finely slice them. If using spinach, simply roughly chop, stems and all. Toss the chopped greens in a bowl with the roughly chopped dill.

Add a lug of olive oil and a few good pinches of salt and pepper to the potatoes and gently toss until well coated. Pick the potatoes up one by one and gently squeeze them between your fingers so they burst open.

Lay out 4 large pieces of parchment paper, approximately 16 x 16 inches. Divide your greens between them and top with some new potatoes. Lay a fillet of fish, skin side up, on top of each pile of veg. Drizzle a tablespoon of white wine vinegar over each fillet, then chop your bunch of chives in half and scatter a few over your fish. Carefully, bring two sides of the paper together over the fish, fold it down a few times, then tuck the paper under at each end.

Pop the parcels on a baking sheet and roast in your hot oven for 18 to 20 minutes, or until the fish is cooked through. Remove from the oven, mix a good pinch of salt and pepper into the sour cream, then spoon into a small serving dish and put on the table. Serve these babies in their parcels so everyone can unwrap their own.

PYTT I PANNA (LITTLE PIECES IN A PAN)

Serves 4

- 6 slices of smoked streaky bacon, the best quality you can afford
- 2 smoked or regular sausages, cooked, the best quality you can afford
- 10½ ounces cooked brisket or other leftover cooked meat
- 3 ounces salami, skin removed
- 2 small onions, peeled
- 3 large carrots, quartered
- 2 pounds potatoes, scrubbed clean
- a few sprigs of fresh rosemary and thyme, leaves picked
- sea salt and freshly ground black pepper
- 4 quail's eggs
- a jar of dill pickles, to serve

For the dressing

- 1 teaspoon good mustard
- 1 tablespoon good-quality cider vinegar
- 3 tablespoons extra virgin olive oil
- a small handful of fresh chives, finely chopped
- a small handful of fresh dill, roughly chopped
- a small handful of fresh flat-leaf parsley, leaves picked

I wish I'd known about this dish earlier in my life, because it's the sort of brilliant everyday dish I absolutely love. Essentially it's a hash. Everyone I spoke to in Sweden seemed to have their preferred method of making theirs; this is mine. The one thing that seems to be consistent is that it usually involves using leftover meat and potatoes. The idea is to chop and slice all the ingredients into roughly 1 inch cubes and add them to the pan as you go. So you're prepping and frying until everything is beautifully cooked. If you want to see how I made this in Sweden, go to www.jamieoliver.com/how-to.

Swedes always serve this topped with a raw egg yolk. That might freak some people out, but you've got to get your head around it because the idea is that you toss it all up yourself and the yolk enriches the whole thing as it slowly gets cooked by the residual heat.

Heat a really wide shallow non-stick pan over medium heat. Chop your bacon into small pieces and fry for 2 to 3 minutes so that the fat starts to render out. While that's happening, chop up your sausage, brisket and salami into cubes, and add to the pan as you go. Do the same with the onions, carrots, potatoes and herbs. Keep stirring to make sure nothing catches, using your spoon to scrape all the goodness from the bottom of the pan. Turn the heat down if you think it's cooking too fast. Have a taste to check the seasoning; the salt in the smoked meats will probably be enough, but add a pinch of salt and a good pinch of pepper if you think it needs it.

Keep stirring as it cooks and after about 20 minutes, once the potatoes and carrots have softened and everything looks delicious, make your dressing by putting all the dressing ingredients into a jar (reserving the dill flowers if you have them). Pour the dressing into the pan - the acidity will be fantastic with all that rich meat. Carefully separate the egg whites from their yolks and put them to one side. If you want to, leave the yolks in their shells so everyone can tip their own egg yolk into their dish and stir it through. That will give the dish a bit of a theatrical edge.

Divide your pytt i panna between the plates. Make a well in the top and add a yolk (or eggshell with a yolk in it) to each one. Load up a side plate with dill pickles, and roughly chop your dill flowers and scatter them over. The combination of meaty comforting hash, egg for sheen, dressing for acidity and herbs for freshness is insane. Go for it!

JANSSON'S TEMPTATION

Serves 6–8 as a side

- 2 pounds potatoes, peeled
- olive oil
- 4 cloves of garlic
- 2 small onions, peeled and finely sliced
- 1 x 2 ounce can of anchovies, drained and finely chopped
- 3 tablespoons butter, plus extra for greasing
- a small bunch of fresh thyme, leaves picked
- zest of 1 lemon
- sea salt and freshly ground black pepper
- 1¼ cups heavy cream
- 1¼ cups milk
- ¼ cup fine breadcrumbs

This is a really popular Swedish dish that's enjoyed either as a late-night snack or as part of a bigger meal. In Sweden they have the most gorgeous anchovies. I don't know what it is, but they seem to be sweeter and more flavorful than the canned ones I'm used to. If you're not a big fan of anchovies that's all right, just use half the amount in this recipe and you'll still end up with a delicious dish. You can eat it on its own, but personally I think it makes a brilliant accompaniment to a roast dinner or other beautifully cooked meat.

Preheat your oven to 400°F. Use the coarse side of a box grater or the julienne attachment of a food processor to grate all your potatoes into a large colander, then use your hands to really scrunch and squeeze them so you get any excess moisture out.

Heat a lug of olive oil in a large frying pan over high heat. While it heats up peel the garlic cloves, then finely slice 3 of them and add to the pan along with your sliced onions. Reduce the heat to low and cook for 4 to 5 minutes, until the onions have softened but not colored. Add the anchovies and stir through for a minute or so, then take the pan off the heat and put to one side.

Meanwhile, crush your remaining garlic clove with the back of a knife and rub it round a wide, shallow earthenware dish (approximately 8½ x 11 inches), then grease the dish well with butter. Spread half the grated potatoes over the bottom of the dish, then scatter over the softened onion mixture, half the thyme leaves and half the lemon zest. Season with black pepper and a little pinch of salt. Top with the rest of your potatoes, spread them out into a nice even layer, then pour over the cream and milk.

Put your breadcrumbs into a bowl with the remaining thyme leaves and lemon zest and a good pinch of salt and pepper. Toss together, then scatter over the potatoes. Dot the butter all over the top, and bake in the hot oven for 45 minutes, with a baking sheet on the shelf beneath to catch any bits that bubble over, until crisp, golden and delicious. Take it straight to the table and serve piping hot, next to any nice roasted meat or fish and some simple greens or a beautiful fresh salad.

My darling Anna is a ball of energy. She became my friend twelve years ago when she ran a Swedish stall at London's Borough Market. She's always been a tireless ambassador for Swedish food, so it was great to see her on her home turf. We spent a wonderful day foraging for wild mushrooms and berries on her brother's island in the archipelago (how cool is that?!).

CREAMY MUSHROOMS

Serves 4

- a small rustic loaf of bread, to serve
- 12 ounces chanterelles
- a small bunch of fresh curly parsley
- 2 tablespoons butter
- olive oil
- ½ a red onion, peeled and finely sliced
- sea salt and freshly ground black pepper
- ⅔ cup half and half
- 1 lemon

This is a small snack or a lovely little starter. Feel free to use this recipe with any good eating mushrooms you can get your hands on. I've noticed that it seems to be compulsory around the world to cook wild mushrooms simply, in a pan with butter, oil, garlic, some sort of herb, salt and pepper. I can't argue with that method - it does give delicious results - but the nice thing about this recipe is that with all the juices that naturally cook out of the mushrooms and mix with the butter, you only need to add a touch of cream to get a sauce that gives the illusion of being really creamy when it's actually not. I think this is best served bubbling in the pan with some chunks of bread, but it could also become a layer in a lasagne, be spooned over steak or pork, get tossed with pasta or be paired with beef strips and rice for a sort of stroganoff. What a treat.

Preheat your oven to its lowest setting and pop the loaf of bread in to warm through. Spend a few minutes gently brushing along the underside of the mushrooms to get rid of any bugs and dirt that might be hiding there. This is well worth the effort. Finely chop your parsley, stalks and all, reserving a few of the leaves.

Put the butter into a large hot pan and as soon as it starts to melt add a drizzle of olive oil, the mushrooms, sliced onion and a good pinch of salt and pepper. Stir everything around and cook for about 8 minutes, or until the onions have softened and the mushrooms are starting to caramelize and take on color.

Add the chopped parsley, then pour in the half and half. Continue to stir and cook for another minute, until the liquid has come to a boil, then turn down the heat and simmer for a minute before removing from the heat. Add a good squeeze of lemon juice, have a taste, and add more salt, pepper or lemon juice if it needs it. Take your bread out of the oven and tear it into big chunks. Divide the mushrooms between your plates and scatter over the reserved parsley leaves. Serve with chunks of bread on the side to mop up all the creamy mushroomy juices, and tuck in!

Even though the crayfish season in Sweden is short, people really make the most of it. In August they throw traditional crayfish parties or "kräftskiva". Like most of the things the Swedes seem to love doing, these parties involve copious amounts of booze and loud singing, as well as plenty of crayfish.

SKAGEN
(SHRIMP ON TOAST)

Serves 4

- 1 pound cooked, peeled shrimp (sustainably caught – see introduction)
- ½ a red onion, peeled and very finely chopped
- ½ a bunch of fresh dill, very finely chopped
- 3 tablespoons extra virgin olive oil
- zest and juice of ½ a lemon
- 4 tablespoons sour cream
- sea salt and freshly ground black pepper
- a loaf of brioche or soft, white bread
- 1½ tablespoons butter, diced
- optional: fish roe, to serve

For all intents and purposes, this dish is the Swedish equivalent of our shrimp cocktail. As much as I love that when it's done properly, the flavor combo of ketchup and mayo isn't the biggest turn-on in the world. This, on the other hand, uses generous amounts of lemon and dill in the mayonnaise and the result is clean, zingy and zippy in flavor – I'd expect nothing less from the Swedes. It involves hardly any work, but if you pile a spoonful of these dressed shrimp on a toasted piece of brioche or sourdough bread you'll have a really confident little light lunch or starter.

Put the shrimp into a bowl with the finely chopped onion, most of the dill, the extra virgin olive oil, lemon zest and juice and sour cream. Season with a couple of good pinches of salt and pepper and gently mix together. Have a taste and check that you've got the right balance of acidity and salt, then put to one side.

Put a large frying pan over high heat. Cut 4 thick slices of brioche or bread and put them into the hot pan, dropping the cubes of butter in and around the bread so it can soak in. Turn the heat down to medium and continue to cook until the slices are toasted on both sides. Put a slice on each plate and spoon over your shrimp. If you've got some good fish roe, add a little spoonful of that on top, then sprinkle over the rest of your dill and serve right away.

Scandinavian countries are great at healthy snacking and
a buffet-style of eating called smörgåsbord ('smörgås' means
open-faced sandwich and 'bord' means table). You can sometimes
find large crispbreads like these in supermarkets or Swedish shops.
But you could easily do something similar by topping Ryvitas
with all sorts of fresh, contrasting textures.

Some cracking combinations: cucumber, horseradish, smoked fish, salmon roe and chives; gravlax and pickled cucumber; shrimp, half a quail's egg and a squeeze of cod's roe; endive, pickled herring, sour cream and dill; mild cheese, pickle, spoonful of lingonberry; mild cheese, rare roast beef and mustard; smoked ham and radish; ham, cherry tomato and chives ... The sky's the limit!

This trip left me with a huge amount of admiration and affection for the Swedish people. They've got this way of living life to the fullest, and a sense of fun, with just a touch of silliness, that makes being there, and being around them, such a pleasure.

SEXY SWEDISH BUNS

Makes 8 buns

For the dough

- 1 x 2¼ teaspoon package of active dry yeast
- 1¾ cups warm milk
- 1 heaped teaspoon ground cardamom (or about 20 cardamom pods)
- 2 large eggs, preferably free-range or organic
- a pinch of sea salt
- ¾ cup plus 1 tablespoon granulated sugar
- 3 tablespoons melted butter
- 6½ cups all-purpose flour, plus extra for dusting
- 1 tablespoon unsalted butter
- ⅓ cup demerara sugar

For the filling

- 14 ounces blueberries
- ⅓ cup plus 1 teaspoon granulated sugar
- 1 orange

Often, when you least expect it, Swedish dishes get spanked by the use of really interesting spices. Cardamom is the sort of flavor you'd expect to taste in Indian food, but they love it in Sweden too. Swedes add eggs and butter to lots of pastries to enrich them, so they've often got a sort of brioche vibe going on, which is a really lovely thing that I've incorporated here. The sourness of the berries really brings out the sweetness of the bread, and on top of that it looks bloody gorgeous. If you want a little guidance on how to make these, go to www.jamieoliver.com/how-to.

Stir the yeast into the warm milk in a bowl, then put it aside. If using cardamom pods, lightly bash them in a pestle and mortar, then pick out the husks and pound the seeds to a fine powder. Beat the eggs and salt in a large bowl, then add the cardamom, sugar, melted butter, 2¼ cups of the flour and the milk and yeast mixture. Whisk constantly as you add everything so you end up with quite a thick, gluey consistency. Mix in the remaining flour until you have a dough. Use clean floured hands to bring the dough together, then dust the top with flour. Cover the bowl with plastic wrap and leave in a warm place to proof for 1 hour, or until the dough has doubled in size and is full of air pockets.

Meanwhile, put the blueberries and granulated sugar into a bowl. Finely grate the orange zest and add most of it to the bowl, along with a good squeeze of orange juice, then mash together with a potato masher. Line a large baking sheet with parchment paper, then dot the paper with a few knobs of the butter and sprinkle over half the demerara sugar.

Dust a clean surface and your hands with flour and gently stretch and pull the risen dough out until it's a bit bigger than an 8 x 11 piece of paper. This next bit is pretty messy, so have a bowl of flour on hand to help you handle the dough and don't be alarmed if it seems quite wet. Use a slotted spoon to move half the mashed blueberries on to the dough. Try not to include too much juice. Use the back of the spoon to spread the blueberries around the dough. Pull the sides of the dough up and into the middle like an envelope, and keep turning and pushing the dough together.

Cut the dough into 8 equal portions, then pull and stretch each one into a long, thin sausage shape, twisting them around on themselves so you get a sort of rough knot. Arrange them on the sheet, leaving enough room between for them to spread as they cook. Push your fingers into the top of each one to make a little well, then spoon in a few of the remaining mashed berries and gently push them down. Spoon over a little of the blueberry juice from the bowl, then sprinkle with the rest of your demerara and the reserved orange zest. Cover with a damp tea towel and leave to proof for about 20 minutes in a warm place.

Preheat your oven to 350°F. Once the buns have risen, put them into the oven and cook for 25 minutes, until golden and crispy. Serve them, hot and delicious.

THE QUICKEST BERRY TART

Serves 12

- 3 tablespoons vanilla sugar, or 3 tablespoons granulated sugar plus 1 tablespoon pure vanilla extract
- 1¾ cups heavy cream
- zest of 1 orange
- 1⅓ pounds mixed seasonal berries, such as blackberries, loganberries, blueberries, red and white currants, good gooseberries
- 4 meringue nests, broken into rough pieces
- confectioners' sugar, for dusting

For the pastry

- 2 cups plus 1½ tablespoons all-purpose flour, plus extra for dusting
- 3 tablespoons confectioners' sugar
- 4½ ounces good-quality unsalted cold butter, cut into small cubes
- 1 large egg, preferably free-range or organic, beaten
- a splash of milk
- olive oil, for greasing the tart tin

Although this recipe is a bit off the wall, the flavors and textures work so well together. Swedes absolutely love berries, and this is basically a berry tart that's crashed into an Eton mess to create an insanely easy and delicious dessert. I can't tell you how quick it is to knock together.

If you're making this for a dinner party and want to work ahead a bit, just bake the pastry a few hours before, whip the cream mixture together and keep it covered in the fridge. Then, when you're ready to serve it, add the fruit and meringues. That way, the meringues will still be crunchy and create an exciting contrast with the soft cream and berries.

You can make your pastry by hand, or in a food processor. From a height, sieve your flour and confectioners' sugar into a large mixing bowl. Using your fingertips, gently work the butter into the flour and sugar until the mixture resembles breadcrumbs. Add the egg and milk and gently work it together using your hands until you have a ball. Don't work the pastry too much or it will become elastic and chewy, not crumbly and short.

Sprinkle some flour over the dough and a clean work surface, and pat the ball into a thick flat round. Sprinkle over a little more flour, then wrap the pastry in plastic wrap and pop it into the fridge to rest for 30 minutes. Lightly oil the inside of a 10 inch non-stick loose-bottomed tart tin. Dust a clean surface and a rolling pin with flour, then carefully roll out your pastry, turning it every so often, until you've got a circle about ¼ inch thick. Roll the pastry over the rolling pin, then unroll it into the tin, making sure you push it into all the sides. Trim off any extra, and use it to patch any holes, then prick the base of the case all over with a fork, cover with plastic wrap, and pop it into the freezer for 30 minutes. Preheat your oven to 350°F.

Lay a large piece of or parchment paper over the pastry, pushing it right into the sides. Fill the paper right up to the top with uncooked rice, and bake for 10 minutes in your hot oven. Take the pan out, carefully remove the rice (save it for baking another pastry base or pie shell) and parchment paper, and return the base to the oven to cook for a further 10 minutes, until it's firm and almost cookie-like. Leave to cool completely.

Whisk 2 tablespoons of vanilla sugar in a bowl with the cream and most of the orange zest until you get a silky mixture that forms soft peaks. Put half your berries into another bowl and use a fork to mash them up with the remaining tablespoon of vanilla sugar. Gently fold the mushed-up berries and the meringue pieces into your cream. Tip the mixture into your cooled tart base and gently shake it to help spread it out to the edges. Use a spatula or the back of a spoon to spread it out evenly, then sprinkle the remaining berries all over the top. Scatter over your remaining orange zest and serve right away, with a dusting of confectioners' sugar.

CURED MEATS Long winters mean **cured and dried meats** are very popular. Reindeer and elk are the most popular and make delicious cured sausages.

CRAYFISH These are similar in taste and texture to lobster. They are simply boiled in salted water with dill flowers, then served whole with melted butter.

MUSTARD AND DILL **Dill** is by far the most popular herb in Sweden. It's used mainly as a garnish, but also to flavor all sorts of cured fish, from herring to gravlax. Swedish **mustard** tends to be sweeter in flavor and less hot than English and French mustards. It is usually served as an accompaniment to cured meats and cheeses.

BERRIES Sweden's many wonderful wild **berries** are used in jellies, jams, syrups and sauces, and are a common accompaniment to cured meats.

PICKLED HERRING Baltic **herring** are pickled in an endless variety of flavors. Often served simply with crispbreads and sour cream.

SCHNAPPS These strong spirits, such as aquavit, are often flavored with caraway seeds, fennel and anise.

CRISPBREADS These are usually made from rye flour and water and come in many shapes and sizes. Lovely with cheese, gravlax or pickled herring.

SPICES Spices like aniseed, allspice berries, cardamom, cinnamon, fennel seeds and caraway are really popular in Sweden. They are used to flavor everything from pickled herring, to wonderful baked and dried breads, to schnapps.

CHEESE Sweden produces many good, mild cow's milk **cheeses**. Västerbotten and Grevé are the most widely known. Commonly served with crispbreads.

SALMON This is one of the most popular fish in the country and is used for the world-famous gravlax (see page 138).

MOROCCO

MOROCCO

Marrakesh ... what a city! The few days I spent there were pretty much a full-on explosion of the senses: the smells, the heat, the color, the sounds ... I'd never been anywhere like it.

For the first few hours I was a bit awestruck. Although I learned loads in each place I visited for this book, the other countries shared so many similarities with my own that I never felt truly out of my element. What made this trip so special for me was that it was completely different, and a real adventure. The medina, or old town, was like nothing I'd ever seen. If you could rub out any sign of phones and satellite dishes, you could easily believe you'd stepped back 200 years. The winding narrow alleys, the street vendors, crowded markets and brightly colored cones of spice are so exciting, and I love that there is a real sense that human hands, not computers, make the country rattle along. There are men working in shops, banging out tin pots, women weaving rugs and dudes knocking out the most painstaking, but genius, breads and pastries.

Every little sector of the city seems to have its own smells going on. One of the things I thought was truly brilliant was their use of communal ovens. Moroccan cooking is still very much based around the fire, which the locals seem to share. I saw kids taking their mum's bread dough to the communal bakery on their way to school so it would be ready a few hours later, and men stoking big ovens where people drop off clay pots called tangias, full of raw ingredients, on their way to work. The coals slow-cook everything in the pot so by the time they are collected they contain the most delicious, sticky stew – dead cheap but lovingly looked after. Makes our take-out joints look a bit sad! I've done a version of a tangia in this chapter because I love the simplicity of it.

Religion is definitely at the heart of the community, and you can't be in Marrakesh for more than a day without being influenced by the song and call of the mosque and feeling the importance it plays in people's everyday lives. Marrakesh feels like a safe and happy place, which is probably why tourists have been going there since the 1920s. These days there are plenty of lovely riads and boutique hotels, but you definitely don't need to stay anywhere fancy to have a great time. There are also loads of posh restaurants, but you can eat just as well, if not better, on the street. Trust me: the street is where it's at for grub.

As you drive away from the beautiful Atlas Mountains and get into towns and communities, there are markets, or souks as the locals call them, absolutely everywhere. They are still key in Morocco – no question. Like a lot of visitors, one of the first places I headed to was the market in Marrakesh's main square, Djemaa el Fna. I've been told it's the busiest market in Africa and I can definitely believe it. At first I thought it was going to be like Leicester Square or Piccadilly Circus in London: the sort of place you wouldn't send a mate who was visiting because it's not what London is all about. But I turned out to be wrong, because although it is geared up for tourists, it still feels really authentic.

At night, all the food stalls come out and the square turns into one giant restaurant, with steam, smoke, street performers and musicians as far as the eye can see. And the best part is that they don't bend their recipes to Western tastes at all. They make hardcore Moroccan grub, and it's so good! Although most countries use spices in their food, it seems as though Marrakesh has every single one I ever knew existed, and they actively use them on a daily basis. You can easily wander round the market and have a meal over the course of a few hours, just picking at one tiny kebab here, a glass of hand-squeezed orange juice there, some delicious little snails or maybe even a veal tongue sandwich. There are countless people making an endless amount of food – it's my idea of heaven and definitely something to take advantage of.

Because the climate is so wonderful for much of the year, the food vendors have great produce to work with. I spent time wandering through a fruit and vegetable market, and although it was fairly earthy and stripped back, the food being sold there was easily on a par with some of the best produce I've seen. The small restaurants all around that market served the people who worked there, and no doubt used their incredible fresh produce. I ate simple but delicious dishes like yellow split pea soup, warm flatbreads and stuffed sandwiches with grilled meats, some of which I've put into this chapter.

Like most other countries in the world, it's the women who are the main cooks in Morocco. They hold the key to all the great family recipes, so I was really lucky to be invited for lunch with a local family. What's lovely is that cooking isn't seen as a chore or a pain; far from it. The women I met saw it as something that gave them power, control and another way of expressing love for their families. It added another layer and texture to my memory of this wonderful country and helped me understand the recipes here much better. It was one of the most exciting cooking experiences I've had – and I can't wait to do it again.

GRILLED SARDINES

Serves 4

- 8 fresh sardines, boned and scaled (sustainably caught – see introduction)
- 2 teaspoons fennel seeds
- ½ teaspoon ground ginger
- ½ teaspoon ground cumin
- sea salt and freshly ground black pepper
- zest and juice of ½ a lemon
- a few sprigs of fresh flat-leaf parsley, finely chopped (stalks and all)
- extra virgin olive oil
- 4 pitas or flatbreads

For the salad

- a large handful of mixed olives, pitted and roughly chopped
- ½ a preserved lemon (p. 216), pulp discarded and rind roughly chopped
- ½ a cucumber, shaved or peeled
- a handful of radishes, trimmed and peeled or finely sliced
- 1 small fennel bulb, shaved or peeled, leafy tops reserved
- 1 small green pepper, deseeded and diced
- juice of 1 lemon

Sardines are really common in this part of the world, and most restaurants will have some version of them on the menu as a starter. The most common ways to enjoy them are to either grill or barbecue them simply, or fry them, then pop them inside sandwiches. I'm using a zingy marinade on the fish before grilling, as a nod to the French influences of Morocco's past. I think the flavors complement each other beautifully. Serve these simply, with a fresh salad and a few flatbreads, and you'll have a wonderful opener to any meal.

If you need to butterfly the sardines yourself, rinse them under the tap, then make sure the cut where they've been gutted goes all the way to the tail. Put them on a board, skin side up, and press down on the spine with the palm of your hand to flatten them out. Turn them over, and you should be able to carefully pull the bones out in one go, trimming them from the tail end with a knife.

Using a pestle and mortar, roughly bash up the fennel seeds with the ginger, cumin, a good pinch of salt and pepper, the lemon zest and parsley. Add a generous lug of extra virgin olive oil to make a paste, then rub this all over your sardines.

Put a grill pan over high heat. Once the pan is really hot, add your sardines, skin side down, and cook for 2 minutes, then flip over, cook for 1 minute on the other side and squeeze in the juice from your zested lemon.

While your sardines are cooking, warm your breads in a hot dry pan for 30 seconds or so. Toss together all your salad ingredients, apart from the lemon juice, with a generous lug of extra virgin olive oil and a good pinch of pepper. Add a good squeeze of lemon juice and have a taste, then keep adjusting the flavors until you're happy. The preserved lemons should add enough saltiness, but add a small pinch of salt if you feel it needs more.

Serve your sardines with any juices from the pan drizzled over, and the lovely salad on the side. Scatter over the reserved fennel tops and serve with the bread to mop up all the juices.

SHRIMP-STUFFED SPICY FISH WITH VERMICELLI

Serves 2

- 3½ ounces vermicelli, or angel hair pasta
- 2 zucchini
- 2 tomatoes, roughly chopped
- a small bunch of fresh cilantro, roughly chopped
- 1 small preserved lemon (or ½ a home-made preserved lemon – see page 216), finely chopped
- a pinch of ground cumin, plus a little extra
- 1 teaspoon sweet paprika, plus a little extra
- 1 teaspoon ground ginger, plus a little extra
- 2 teaspoons harissa
- sea salt and freshly ground black pepper
- 2 x 10½ ounce dorade, or other large fish such as sea bass, snapper or cod, scaled, fins cut off, cavity cut open and cleaned (sustainably caught – see introduction)
- olive oil
- a large handful of small raw peeled shrimp (sustainably caught – see introduction)

This is my version of a wonderful dish I saw being made in a restaurant run by a woman in Marrakesh. It's impressive, tasty, and perfect for a dinner party. You can use any fish with a large cavity as long as it's fresh and in season. Although I used one large fish in Morocco, it's not always that easy to get your hands on one that size, so I've given you a recipe for two smaller ones here. If you are able to get a lovely big fish, like sea bass or snapper, this dish will be a triumph. Just turn the heat down to 350°F and cook until the meat flakes off the bone.

Preheat your oven to 400°F. Bring a pan of salted water to the boil, add the vermicelli, and cook for slightly less time than it says on the packet. You want it to be al dente. Once ready, drain, rinse in cold water and leave to cool. Put it into a large bowl and grate in your zucchini. Add the chopped tomatoes, cilantro, preserved lemon, cumin, sweet paprika, ground ginger and 1 teaspoon of harissa. Mix it all together really well with your clean hands, then have a taste, add a pinch of salt and pepper if needed, and put aside.

Place the fish on a large chopping board and score the skin every ¾ inch on both sides at a slight angle, using a sharp knife. Sprinkle over a little salt, a small pinch of cumin, and a pinch each of sweet paprika and ground ginger. Mix the remaining teaspoon of harissa with 1 teaspoon of olive oil and rub half of it into the fish, making sure it gets into the cuts you've made. Turn the fish over and repeat on the other side.

Spoon two-thirds of your vermicelli filling into a large baking pan or earthenware-type dish, making a bed for the fish, and gently place the fish on top. Stir your shrimp into the rest of the vermicelli filling and spoon this into the cavity of your fish, pushing it right in - don't worry if it spills out a little. Drizzle over a little olive oil, and roast in the hot oven for around 25 minutes, until the fish is crisp on the outside and cooked through.

To serve, pull the meat off and pick the bones out. Add a spoonful of the vermicelli filling on the side of each plate and serve with a crisp dressed green salad.

P.S. Any leftover vermicelli will be delicious the next day as a cold salad.

When in Morocco, or any country, if you're into food and like getting up early, find out where the commercial food markets are and just turn up. You'll discover great restaurants nearby, the most incredible produce, and lovely people to meet. You can learn so much about a country by spending an hour or two this way – it's well worth the early alarm!

RATATOUILLE-STYLE BRIOUATS

Serves 4

- 2 ripe tomatoes, halved
- 2 zucchini, halved lengthways and sliced
- 1 onion, peeled and cut into 8 wedges
- 1 red pepper, deseeded and roughly chopped
- 1 eggplant, halved lengthways and sliced
- 2 cloves of garlic, peeled and crushed
- olive oil
- sea salt and freshly ground black pepper
- 2 teaspoons ras el hanout spice mix (see page 226)
- 2 lemons
- 8 sheets of phyllo pastry (or 4 sheets of warkha pastry)
- 1 tablespoon extra virgin olive oil
- ⅔ cup Greek yogurt
- 2 teaspoons harissa
- a few sprigs of fresh flat-leaf parsley

Briouats are hand-held pastry parcels full of all sorts of beautiful things. They are sold at street markets and are made with a delicious pastry called warkha, which you can see being handmade all over Marrakesh by really talented guys. Some specialty stores and online sources in the US sell warkha, also known as brick pastry ("feuilles de brick"). Although slightly more robust than phyllo pastry, warkha looks and behaves quite similarly, so I'm using phyllo instead because it's so accessible. If you want to see how these lovely briouats are assembled, go to www.jamieoliver.com/how-to.

You'll find a huge range of fillings in briouats, from sweet to savory. I've gone for a vegetarian concept here, because I love the contrast between delightful, delicious cooked veggies and the crisp golden pastry.

Preheat your oven to 325°F. Put the prepared vegetables and crushed garlic onto a large baking sheet. Drizzle over a good few of lugs olive oil and season generously with salt and pepper. Scatter over the ras el hanout, then toss together so that everything is well coated. Cook in the hot oven for 45 minutes, tossing everything halfway through, until the vegetables are cooked and lovely and golden. Remove from the oven and leave to cool, then roughly chop all the vegetables into small chunks and put them into a large bowl. Squeeze over the juice from one of your lemons and mix well. Have a taste to check the seasoning, then put aside.

Lay 2 sheets of phyllo pastry on top of each other. Divide the filling into 4, then spoon one portion along the length of the pastry, leaving a small gap at either end. Roll up so you get a long cigar shape. When you're halfway through, fold in the ends and keep going. Do this until you have 4 rolls.

Put about ¼ inch of olive oil into a large frying pan and place it over medium heat. After about 5 minutes, the oil should be nice and hot, so use a slotted spoon to carefully add the briouts to the pan and fry them for about 4 to 5 minutes, turning on all sides, until golden brown. Keep an eye on the pan, as hot oil is very dangerous.

Meanwhile, mix the extra virgin olive oil and yogurt together in a small bowl. Swirl in the harissa and top with a pinch of pepper.

Once your briouats are cooked, use a slotted spoon to carefully move them onto a plate lined with paper towels to drain. Finely chop your parsley, and serve the briouats right away with a pinch of black pepper and chopped parsley scattered over and the gorgeous harissa dip on the side. Lovely with a crisp green salad and some lemon wedges for squeezing over.

P.S. If you're not keen on frying these you could always pop them on a baking sheet and bake them until crisp and golden at 375°F.

I loved this market, Djemaa el Fna, and there are many others like it in Marrakesh. At five o'clock, the vendors bundle out of their lock-ups and set up these cooking stalls. The food is ridiculously good and cheap and the atmosphere is fantastic. It's a brilliant way to spend an evening.

KEFTA (LOVELY MEATBALLS)

Serves 4

- 1 small red onion, peeled and finely sliced
- 2 handfuls of cherry tomatoes, halved
- juice of ½ a lemon
- extra virgin olive oil
- olive oil
- 4 pitas or flatbreads
- Greek yogurt, to serve
- harissa, to serve
- 4 handfuls of mixed salad leaves

For the kefta

- 1 pound ground beef
- 1 small red onion, peeled and finely grated
- 1 teaspoon ground cumin
- 1 teaspoon ground coriander
- 1 teaspoon paprika
- ½ a thumb-sized piece of fresh ginger, peeled and finely grated
- a small bunch of fresh cilantro, finely chopped
- sea salt and freshly ground black pepper

You'll see these spicy little meatballs being sold at street stalls all over Marrakesh. They are yet another great example of what good Moroccan street food is all about. Start with simple ground meat – I'm using beef, but lamb would be delicious and authentic – then add personality with delicious spices, and cook simply, adding flashes and slaps of exciting flavor from lemony dressed greens, thinly sliced onion and spicy chile sauce. Whether you have them for lunch or dinner they will hit the spot, because any time you have stacks of piping hot meatballs and piles of flatbreads to stuff them into you're in for a treat.

If you're using a grill, light it now so it can get good and hot. Put all the kefta ingredients into a big bowl and season generously with salt and pepper. Use your clean hands to really scrunch and mix everything together. Divide the mixture into quarters, then divide each quarter into 5 meatballs. Place them on a tray, cover with plastic wrap and pop into the fridge for at least 30 minutes.

If you're using a grill pan or a large non-stick frying pan, get it over medium heat when you take the kefta out of the fridge. Put the finely sliced red onion and halved cherry tomatoes into a small bowl. Add the lemon juice and twice as much extra virgin olive oil, and toss together until nicely dressed. Have a taste, season with salt and pepper if needed, then pop to one side.

Drizzle the kefta with a little olive oil, then either grill them or cook them in your hot pan, turning occasionally for about 7 to 10 minutes, or until cooked through and nicely charred. You might need to do this in two batches so you don't overcrowd the pan. Meanwhile, warm your breads in a hot dry pan for 30 seconds or so on each side.

Tear your warm breads in half, then slit them open with a knife. Spoon and spread some yogurt and harissa into the open bread, and add a spoonful of red onion salad and a couple of kefta to each. Serve with salad leaves on the side and go for it. Absolutely delicious!

MOROCCAN FISH AND CHIPS

Serves 4

- 1⅓ pounds monkfish tails, skin off, trimmed and cut into 2 inch pieces (sustainably caught – see introduction)
- olive oil
- sea salt and freshly ground black pepper
- 2 pounds baking potatoes, scrubbed clean
- olive oil
- 2 ripe tomatoes, roughly chopped
- ½ a small cucumber, halved lengthways and finely sliced
- 1 carrot, peeled and cut into matchsticks or peeled into strips
- 1 tablespoon capers, drained
- a small bunch of fresh cilantro, leaves picked
- 4 pitas or flatbreads
- 1 tablespoon white wine vinegar
- 3 tablespoons extra virgin olive oil
- natural yogurt, to serve

For the marinade

- ½ tablespoon paprika
- ½ tablespoon turmeric
- ½ tablespoon ground ginger
- ½ tablespoon ground coriander
- a small bunch of fresh flat-leaf parsley, finely chopped

This is a really simple thing to knock out - and you can experiment with dry and wet rubs until you find a combination of spices that really works for you. I've added chips because I love the idea of this dish being a cross between home, because of the chips, and away, thanks to the fish being flavored with exotic spices. The monkfish will take just a few minutes, so get your chips golden and just about ready to eat, then pop the pieces of fish on the grill or grill pan and get everyone round the table, ready to tuck in.

P.S. If you're cooking these on a grill, just remember that it will need to be screaming hot, so give yourself enough time to light it and get it up to temperature.

Preheat the oven to 400°F. Put your monkfish into a bowl with all the marinade ingredients, 2 tablespoons of olive oil and a nice big pinch of salt and pepper. Mix well so that the monkfish gets evenly coated, then cover with plastic wrap and refrigerate for at least 1 hour.

Meanwhile, cut the potatoes into ½ inch thick chips and spread out in a single layer on 2 large baking sheets. Drizzle over a few lugs of olive oil, season well with salt and pepper, and toss the chips until coated. Roast for about 30 to 40 minutes, or until cooked through, crisp and lightly golden. Halfway through the cooking time, swap the sheets around in the oven and give each one a good shake so all the chips cook evenly.

Put a grill pan or large non-stick frying pan on a high heat to get really hot. Make your salad by mixing the tomatoes, cucumber, carrot, capers and cilantro together in a bowl.

About 10 minutes before your chips are ready to come out of the oven, put your monkfish pieces into the screaming hot pan and cook, turning every couple of minutes, for 5 to 7 minutes, until firm and cooked through. You'll need to do this in two batches if you have a small pan. Warm your breads in a hot dry pan for 30 seconds or so on each side, or wrap them in foil and pop them into the oven for a few minutes. Dress your salad with the white wine vinegar and extra virgin olive oil, then season with a pinch of salt and pepper and toss.

Tear your warm breads in half and slit them open with a knife. Stuff the pockets with a small handful of salad, a few monkfish chunks and a dollop of yogurt. Sprinkle a little paprika over your chips and serve on the side.

CHICKEN KEBABS WITH AVOCADO DIP

Serves 4

- 4 boneless chicken breasts (approximately 4½ ounces each), preferably free-range or organic, cut into bite-sized chunks
- 4 pitas or flatbreads
- 1 lemon, cut into wedges, to serve

For the marinade

- a thumb-sized piece of fresh ginger, peeled and finely grated
- 1 tablespoon hot paprika
- 1 teaspoon turmeric
- 1 teaspoon ground coriander
- 3 tablespoons olive oil
- sea salt and freshly ground black pepper

For the avocado dip

- 2 ripe avocados
- 1 teaspoon ground cumin
- 2 cloves of garlic, peeled and very finely chopped
- 1 fresh green or red chile, deseeded and finely chopped
- a small bunch of fresh cilantro, finely chopped
- 2 tablespoons extra virgin olive oil
- juice of 1 lemon

Nothing could be simpler to knock out than these chicken skewers. Again, you've got wonderful warm flatbreads as the carrier for hot delicious meat cooked simply on a grill. Although the fresh avocado dip here isn't typically Moroccan, the smooth and silky texture spiked with chile really complements the sizzling chicken kebabs. I've used chicken breasts here, because they're quicker to cook and people seem to buy them more often, but if I were making these at home I'd probably go for skinless, boneless chicken thighs and cook them on a slightly lower heat for 5 or 10 minutes more. The breasts will be delicious, but if you have the inclination to spend a bit more time and effort, the thigh meat will reward you by being slightly stickier and more melt-in-the-mouth. You'll get amazing results if you marinate these overnight before grilling them.

Another thing I'll say is that every house should have twenty metal skewers. It might sound a bit geeky, but you just need to buy them once and they'll see you through the rest of your life. I think there is something quite spectacular about a load of kebabs lined up by a grill or pan, waiting to be cooked.

Mix all the marinade ingredients in a bowl with a good pinch of salt and pepper. Toss the chicken chunks in the marinade until evenly coated, then cover the bowl with plastic wrap and refrigerate for at least 30 minutes - longer if possible.

Meanwhile, make your avocado dip. Halve your avocados, get rid of the stones, and spoon the flesh into a bowl. Add all the other dip ingredients and a pinch of salt and pepper, and mash well with a fork or a potato masher. You can make this really smooth, or rustic and chunky, it's up to you. I like mine somewhere in the middle. Have a taste to check the seasoning, then put aside.

When you're ready to cook, divide the marinated chicken chunks between your skewers, then get a grill pan over a medium heat. Once it's really hot, add your chicken skewers and cook for 5 to 7 minutes, turning occasionally, until cooked through and golden, with lovely char marks. While that's happening, warm your breads through in another hot dry pan for about 30 seconds per side.

Tear your breads in half, then slit them open with a knife. Dollop the gorgeous avocado dip into the pockets and top with a few pieces of chicken. Serve with lemon wedges on the side for squeezing over.

Keep your eyes open for the mechoui men. These boys cook up to twenty whole lambs at a time in their underground ovens. Once the lambs are slow-roasted to perfection, they're pulled up by the scruff of the spits and turned into stupidly delicious sandwiches.

MECHOUI LAMB WITH CARROT AND ORANGE SALAD

Serves 4
(with lots of lamb left over)

- 1 shoulder of lamb (approximately 5½ pounds)
- 3 tablespoons smen or butter, at room temperature
- 1 heaped teaspoon ground cumin, plus extra to serve
- 1 heaped teaspoon ground coriander, plus extra to serve
- 1 teaspoon sea salt
- a small handful of fresh thyme sprigs, leaves picked
- a few sprigs of fresh rosemary, leaves picked
- freshly ground black pepper
- 1 bulb of garlic
- 4 flatbreads
- seeds from ½ a pomegranate
- 1 cup Greek yogurt
- 4 tablespoons harissa

For the carrot and orange salad
- 4 small carrots, peeled
- juice of ½ an orange
- extra virgin olive oil
- red wine vinegar
- a small bunch of fresh mint, leaves picked, larger ones torn
- sea salt and freshly ground black pepper

I'm really proud of this beautiful dish. I'm not sure what the mechoui man I met in the market in Marrakesh would make of it, but I like to think I'm respecting the way he cooks, by using local ingredients, and linking it back with touches like the carrot and orange salad. What's great is that you can easily make this dish at home and totally get that authentic taste of Morocco. The only thing you might not be able to get hold of is smen, a type of fermented butter, but the regular stuff will work just fine.

Preheat your oven as high as it will go. Place the lamb shoulder in a large roasting pan, skin side up. Rub your smen or butter all over the meat until completely covered, then sprinkle over your cumin and coriander. Pound your salt and thyme leaves in a pestle and mortar and rub all those flavors all over the lamb, along with the rosemary leaves and a few good pinches of pepper.

Smash your garlic bulb open, separate the cloves and push them into the butter on the lamb. Pour around ½ cup of water into the pan and snugly cover the lamb with a double layer of foil. Put the pan into your hot oven and immediately turn the temperature down to 350°F. You'll need to cook a shoulder this size for around 3 hours in total. Remove the foil for the last 30 minutes of cooking. When the skin is nice and crisp and the meat is falling off the bone and deliciously tender, it's ready.

Leave to rest for 10 to 15 minutes, covered loosely with the foil. While it's resting, make the salad. Using a peeler or mandoline, or the grater or julienne cutter of your food processor if you've got one, shred your carrots as finely as possible into a bowl. Dress them with the orange juice, a good lug of extra virgin olive oil, a splash of red wine vinegar, the mint leaves and a pinch of salt and pepper, then toss and take to the table or divide between your plates.

Use forks to shred the lamb. Warm your flatbreads in the oven or a hot dry pan for 30 seconds or so on each side until warm and soft, then sort of scrunch each one into a rough cone shape, like in the picture. Lift up the top pocket so you can stuff in some lamb, and top with a few pomegranate seeds. Dollop some yogurt on the side of the plate, drizzle with a little harissa and a pinch of cumin and coriander and you've got a killer meal.

CHICKEN, OLIVE AND PRESERVED LEMON TAGINE

Serves 4-6

- 1 whole chicken (approximately 3⅓ pounds), preferably free range or organic, skin-on, cut into 4 pieces (get your butcher to do this for you)
- olive oil
- 1-2 large bulbs of fennel
- 2 onions, peeled and roughly chopped
- a small bunch of fresh cilantro
- 4 cloves of garlic, peeled and sliced
- 2-3 small preserved lemons (or 1 home-made preserved lemon – see page 216), deseeded and chopped
- ⅓ cup black and green olives, pitted
- a good pinch of saffron
- 2 cups hot organic chicken stock

For the spice rub

- 1 heaped teaspoon coriander seeds, bashed up
- 1 teaspoon ground cumin
- 1 heaped teaspoon ground ginger
- 2 tablespoons olive oil
- sea salt and freshly ground black pepper

The word "tagine" refers not only to the dish itself, but also to the unique pot it's cooked in. These thick earthenware pots are used all over Morocco and were introduced by nomads, who would use them directly over fire and ashes to create all sorts of beautiful stews with goat, lamb and chicken. Traditionally, the lady of the house would be in charge of cooking the tagine, and that is still very much the way it is today. Apparently, that's one of the ways they express their love and affection. So a word to the wise - if your missus feeds you a dodgy-tasting tagine, look out!

Making this dish in a proper tagine definitely adds to the beauty of it, but essentially it's a stew with deep, lovely flavors and you can still get an authentic taste using a conventional heavy-based casserole pan. I think this recipe delivers every time, and it really makes good use of one of the star flavors in tagines: preserved lemons. You can buy these, but if you want to make your own - and I think you should - check out the recipe on page 216.

Mix all the spice rub ingredients together in a small bowl. Put your chicken pieces into a large bowl, massage them with the spice rub then cover with plastic wrap and put into the fridge to marinate for a couple of hours or, even better, overnight.

When you're ready to cook, heat a generous lug of olive oil in a tagine or casserole-type pan and fry the chicken pieces over medium to high heat, skin side down first, for about 5 to 10 minutes until gorgeous and golden brown.

While your chicken fries, chop each fennel bulb into 8 wedges and add these to the pan along with the onions, cilantro stalks and garlic. Stir well and fry for a couple more minutes, then mix in the preserved lemons, olives and saffron. Pour in the hot stock, give everything a good stir, then cover with a lid or foil and simmer on a low heat for 1½ hours, or until the meat starts to fall away from the bone. Halfway through, have a check and give it a good stir. Keep an eye on it and add a splash of water if it looks dry.

When the time's up and your chicken looks perfect, stir gently. If it's still a bit liquidy, leave it to blip away with the lid off until thickened slightly. Have a taste, season with a pinch of salt and pepper if you think it needs it, then sprinkle with the cilantro leaves. There's enough love and care in the tagine for it not to need anything fancy, so serve it simply, with a large bowl of lightly seasoned steaming couscous.

BEEF TAGINE

Serves 4-6
- 1½ pounds stewing beef
- olive oil
- 1 onion, peeled and finely chopped
- a small bunch of fresh cilantro
- 1 x 14 ounce can of chickpeas, drained
- 1 x 14 ounce can of chopped tomatoes
- 3½ cups vegetable stock, preferably organic
- 1 small squash (approximately 1½ pounds), deseeded and cut into 2 inch chunks
- 3½ ounces prunes, pitted and roughly torn
- 2 tablespoons sliced almonds, toasted

For the spice rub
- sea salt and freshly ground black pepper
- 1 tablespoon ras el hanout spice mix (see page 226)
- 1 tablespoon ground cumin
- 1 tablespoon ground cinnamon
- 1 tablespoon ground ginger
- 1 tablespoon sweet paprika

I like to think of a tagine as a sort of stew with attitude. It's really all about the spices and the slow cooking, giving all the wonderful flavors time to develop. What's great is that you don't need an authentic Moroccan tagine in order to recreate this beautiful food - a saucepan will still give you great results. Having been to Marrakesh and learned all the principles, I now feel I'll be able to rustle up an endless variety of tagines at home. Give this one a try and you'll see what I mean.

Mix all the spice rub ingredients together in a small bowl. Put the beef into a large bowl, massage it with the spice rub, then cover with plastic wrap and put into the fridge for a couple of hours - ideally overnight. That way the spices really penetrate and flavor the meat.

When you're ready to cook, heat a generous lug of olive oil in a tagine or casserole-type pan and fry the meat over a medium heat for 5 minutes. Add your chopped onion and cilantro stalks and fry for another 5 minutes. Tip in the chickpeas and tomatoes, then pour in half of the stock and stir. Bring to the boil, then put the lid on the pan or cover with foil and reduce to a simmer for 1½ hours.

At this point add your squash, the prunes and the rest of the stock. Give everything a gentle stir, then pop the lid back on the pan and continue cooking for another 1½ hours. Keep an eye on it and add a splash of water if it looks too dry.

Once the time is up, take the lid off and check the consistency. If it seems a bit too runny, simmer for 5 to 10 minutes more with the lid off. The beef should be really tender and flaking apart now, so have a taste and season with a pinch or two of salt. Scatter the cilantro leaves over the tagine along with the toasted almonds, then take it straight to the table with a big bowl of lightly seasoned couscous and dive in.

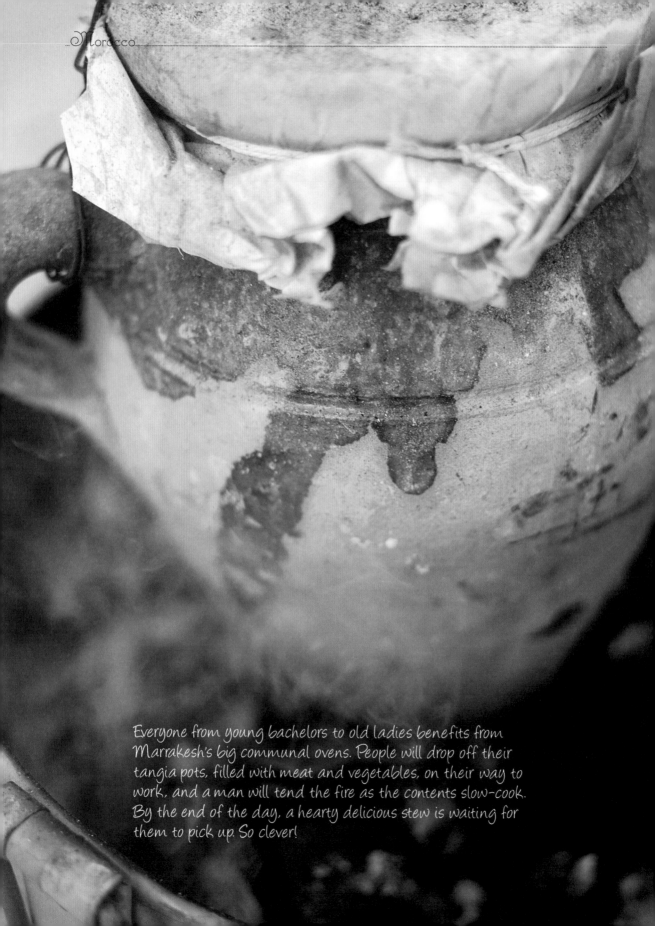

Everyone from young bachelors to old ladies benefits from Marrakesh's big communal ovens. People will drop off their tangia pots, filled with meat and vegetables, on their way to work, and a man will tend the fire as the contents slow-cook. By the end of the day, a hearty delicious stew is waiting for them to pick up. So clever!

SIMPLE LAMB TANGIA

Serves 4-6

- a small handful of mixed olives, unpitted
- 2 small preserved lemons (or 1 home-made preserved lemon – see page 216), roughly chopped
- olive oil
- a large pinch of saffron
- 2 carrots, roughly chopped
- 2 leeks, trimmed and roughly chopped
- ¾ pound baby new potatoes
- 1 bulb of garlic, unpeeled, cloves separated and crushed with the back of a knife
- 1¾ pounds lamb shoulder, cut into 4 inch pieces
- 2 tablespoons smen (fermented butter) or butter
- sea salt and freshly ground black pepper

Traditionally, tangias are slow-cooked in embers over several hours. What's brilliant about them is that you're basically just layering up simple ingredients and letting the heat do all the work. One-pot cooking is really popular in Morocco, particularly among the bachelors! You can easily replicate it at home, and this is a simple recipe to get you started. Moroccans would chop the lamb up, bone and all, but I've used lamb shoulder here to make it less fiddly. When it all cooks down it's just as delicious. If you haven't got an authentic tangia don't worry, you can make this in any large earthenware or casserole-type dish with a tight lid.

Preheat your oven to 300°F. Put the olives and chopped lemons into your tangia first, with a good lug of olive oil and the saffron, and top with all your vegetables, garlic cloves and chunks of lamb. Add the smen or butter and a good pinch of salt and pepper, then pour in about 3 cups of water so everything is just covered. If you don't have a traditional tangia pot, just mix your ingredients together in a bowl then add to a large pan before adding the water.

Cover with a lid or tightly with foil and cook for around 3½ hours in your preheated oven, or until the lamb is tender and falling apart. Serve with warm flatbreads and a lovely fresh salad. Remind people to look out for olive pits as they eat, and make sure everyone squeezes those delicious sticky cloves of garlic out of their skins as they tuck in.

P.S. This same recipe can be made using many other meats, including game or chicken.

PRESERVED LEMONS

- 10 small unwaxed lemons
- ¾ cup coarse sea salt
- 2 fresh bay leaves
- 7 black peppercorns
- 2 sticks of cinnamon

These are a really exciting Moroccan thing to make. They're dead simple, and although this genius ingredient sounds unusual, it really adds the most fantastic zing and freshness to dishes. At first our Western palates might be unsure about them, but it won't take long for you to understand their magic. Just remember, you definitely don't want to eat them out of the jar like you would pickled onions!

Just experiment with them. They add such an exciting layer of flavor that I'm sure you'll find all sorts of great ways to use yours. Whenever you need one, just spoon it out of the jar!

Deseed and finely chop them, then add to rice dishes, salad dressings, stews, tagines ... A tiny bit of preserved lemon over roasted fish is beautiful, as is a mixture of olive, feta and preserved lemon stuffed inside a chicken breast then wrapped in prosciutto and roasted. Yum!

Start by sterilizing a 1 quart Mason jar. It's dead easy. Preheat your oven to 225°F, then put the jar and lid into the oven. Leave for 20 minutes. Remove the lid and the jar from the oven, taking care not to touch anywhere near the opening, then leave to cool completely before preparing the lemons.

Squeeze the juice from 5 of your lemons into a jug and put to one side. Cut a deep cross into the top of each of the remaining lemons and keep going so they're cut through about three-quarters of the way down and the lemons stay joined at the base. Pack a teaspoon of sea salt inside each one, then push the lemons back together. Pop them into your sterilized jar, layering them up with the rest of the salt, the bay leaves, peppercorns and cinnamon sticks. Pour in the lemon juice, then top the jar right up with water. Put the lid on and seal tightly. Leave for a month or so in a cool dark place, giving the jar a gentle shake every few days to move the salt around.

After a month, the preserved lemons will be ready to use in any of the things I've mentioned in the intro or anything else you think will be delicious. They'll keep for ages once they're preserved but if I'm honest, I always use them up within a week or two because I can't wait to try them out in whatever I happen to be cooking.

The ritual and care that goes into brewing Morocco's national drink, mint tea, is a wonderful thing to see. Restaurants buy their fresh mint daily from the markets and serve it sweetened with sugar in the prettiest little glasses.

M'HANNCHA WITH DATE SAUCE

Serves 12

For the m'hanncha

- 13 ounces butter, at room temperature, plus extra for greasing and brushing
- 3⅓ cups confectioners' sugar, plus extra for dusting
- 3 large eggs, preferably free-range or organic
- 2¼ cups ground almonds
- 1 heaped tablespoon all-purpose flour
- zest of 1 lemon
- zest of 1 orange
- 3 tablespoons shelled pistachios, crushed in a pestle and mortar
- 4 tablespoons rose water
- 10 sheets of phyllo pastry
- optional: 3 tablespoons rose petals
- good-quality vanilla ice cream or plain yogurt, to serve

For the date sauce

- 5½ ounces dates, pitted and roughly chopped
- 2 cups freshly squeezed orange juice

Ahhh, the snake! This is an interesting traditional thing I was taught to make in Marrakesh and the sort of dessert that will get a lot of attention when you put it in the middle of the table. It's exotic, dramatic and absolutely delicious: crisp pastry and a comforting, scrumptious, fluffy almond filling spiked with nuts, vanilla and rose water, all rolled up to create the most amazing texture and served with a lovely sticky sauce. It looks like an involved recipe but after you've made it once it will be much faster to do. It's worth it!

Preheat your oven to 350°F. Cream together your butter and confectioners' sugar in a large bowl until really well combined, then gently fold in your eggs, one by one. The mixture will look as though it's curdled, but don't worry. Add the ground almonds and flour and mix well. Finally, stir in the lemon and orange zest, crushed pistachios and rose water.

Lay your phyllo sheets out on a large clean surface in a long line, with the shorter edges towards you. Overlap them by a few inches on each side – you want the line to be around 6½ feet in length. If you've got an extra sheet left in the pack, save it. As evenly as possible, spoon your filling in a long line along the long edge closest to you, leaving about a 3 inch border all the way along on that edge. Scatter over half the rose petals, if using.

Grease a 12 inch round cake pan or a baking sheet with a knob of butter and put aside. Carefully, starting at one end, fold the shorter edge of pastry closest to you over the filling. Do this all the way along so the filling is covered, then gently roll it, nice and tightly, as if you're making a jelly roll, until you have one long sausage. Work quickly, as you don't want the pastry to dry out. If it looks like it might, brush it with a little melted butter to help it along. Tuck the ends in, then roll it again, as tightly as possible, this time to look like a large pinwheel. Gently and carefully slide it off the table on to a plate or a flat board, then slide it from there into your pan or on to your sheet. If you've saved an extra sheet of pastry, use that to patch up any gaps now. Bake for around 40 to 45 minutes, or until gorgeous, crisp and golden. About 15 minutes before the m'hanncha is ready to come out of the oven, start making the date sauce.

Put the dates and orange juice into a small pan and bring to the boil, then reduce to a simmer and cook for 20 minutes. Leave to cool a little, then blitz in a food processor or blender until you have a lovely and smooth but thick sauce.

Take the m'hanncha out of the oven and leave to cool for 10 to 15 minutes. Dust with confectioner's sugar and sprinkle over the remaining rose petals, if using. Serve a wedge of m'hanncha drizzled with the lovely date sauce and a good scoop of vanilla ice cream or plain yogurt on the side.

SWEET COUSCOUS

Serves 4

- 7 ounces dried apricots, pitted and roughly chopped
- 1 orange
- 1 cup plus 2 tablespoons couscous
- 2¼ cups whole milk
- 3 tablespoons runny honey
- a handful of pistachios, shelled
- ground cinnamon

Couscous is one of Morocco's staple ingredients, and although lots of us are familiar with it, we don't tend to think of it as something we'd make a dessert with. But really, couscous is a carrier of flavors, and if you can just get yourself in the right headspace and treat it a bit differently, you'll find it can be used in loads of different ways. Moroccans fluff it up and toss it with fruit and fresh mint, but I'm looking at it almost like porridge and adding some fruit and nut elements to it for a warming oozy pudding. Give it a go and I guarantee you'll find many new ways of using couscous.

Put the chopped apricots into a bowl, add the zest of your orange and just enough boiling water to cover them, and put to one side. Put the couscous into a medium pan over a medium heat and add the milk and 2 tablespoons of the honey. Bring to a simmer, and let it blip away for around 5 to 7 minutes, stirring occasionally. Keep an eye on it and add a splash of water if it looks dry – don't overcook it, as you want it to have a fairly wet consistency still.

Meanwhile, toast the pistachios in a hot dry pan for a few minutes, tossing them occasionally until they start to smell fantastic, and drizzling over the remaining tablespoon of honey near the end so the pistachios go lovely and sticky. Just before you're ready to serve everything, tip the apricots and their juices from the bowl into a blender. Squeeze in the juice from half your orange and whiz to a purée. If it's a bit thick, add the juice from your remaining half orange and whiz again. If you don't have a blender, just spoon the apricots out of the bowl and mush them, then mix this back into the juices until you have a vibrant, fresh apricot compote.

Divide the sweet couscous between four bowls, add a good tablespoon of compote, and spoon over some sticky pistachios. Hit each bowl with a pinch of cinnamon and tuck in straight away!

PAPRIKA, CUMIN AND HARISSA

Ground **paprika** is one of the most widely used spices in Moroccan cooking. It makes an appearance in most spice mixes, including **ras el hanout** (Arabic for "top of the shop"), which is one of the most famous.

It is a blend of the best spices a vendor has in his shop. The mixture varies depending on who is selling it, but it can be a combination of anywhere from 10 to 100 spices. It usually includes nutmeg, cinnamon, mace, aniseed, turmeric, cayenne, peppercorns, dried galangal, ginger, cloves, cardamom, chile, allspice and orris root.

Cumin is used heavily in Moroccan cooking. The seeds are ground and added to tagines, meatballs (kefta) and most grilled meats, and sprinkled over salads and vegetables.

Harissa is a hot red sauce or paste made from smoked chiles and garlic. It's usually used as a base for stews, in meat marinades, or for flavoring couscous.

MINT Morocco has a real love affair with **mint**, and many beautiful varieties are sold in the markets. People buy their fresh mint on a daily basis for the national drink, mint tea.

LAMB **Lamb** is one of the most popular meats in Morocco. Lamb shoulder is used in tagines, and whole lamb is often slow-cooked. Mechoui lamb is roasted over an open fire and is the star celebratory dish of Morocco.

There's a wonderful array of lamb tagines in Morocco that use every vegetable you could name, as well as the dried fruits of the area.

FAVA BEANS, OLIVES AND DATES

Fava beans are used for *bassara*, a popular soup. Fresh fava beans are used in salads.

Moroccan **olives** and Moroccan olive oil give a really distinct, powerful flavor to Moroccan cuisine. They range in color from green to pink and black. The cracked green olives are mostly used in chicken and fish dishes, or as a snack.

There are many dried fruits in Morocco, and **dates** are one of the most common. They come in all shapes and sizes and vary in sweetness. They are used all over North Africa and the Middle East to add sweetness to everything from meat dishes to desserts. The large, chewy, sweet *medjool* dates are considered the best dates in Morocco.

COUSCOUS **Couscous** is a staple in the Moroccan diet. The most common variety is made with semolina granules coated in wheat flour then steamed in a special pot, which is usually placed over a tagine. Traditionally couscous is eaten as part of a Friday lunch, never in the evening, and is served on a platter with tagines or other meat stews, and eaten with the hands.

PRESERVED LEMONS **Preserved lemons** are pickled in salt and are a unique Moroccan ingredient (see page 216). They can be bought in markets and stores all over Morocco. You use either the rind or the pulp, and both if you want a very intense lemon flavor. The rind is finely chopped and added to salads, while the more intense pulp is used to flavor tagines and other stews.

GREECE

GREECE

Years ago, before I knew anything about Greek food, or knew any Greek people, I did a school project on the Acropolis. I may not have come top of the class, but that didn't mean I wasn't full of excitement when I finally arrived in Athens and caught a glimpse of it on the horizon.

Although this was my first trip to Athens, I already had really warm feelings about Greece because of a holiday Jools and I had taken on the island of Crete. It was our first holiday together and we had a wonderful time, thanks to the people. This trip was no different: the people I met were outrageously friendly, sociable, happy and, most of all, so proud to be Greek!

One of the things that immediately struck me about Athens was the way its big ancient buildings are part of, and seem quite at home in, such a busy modern city. It feels utterly chaotic, but in a nice way. That mixture of old and new shows up in its food culture too. There are some fantastic indoor markets that have an almost ancient vibe to them, in the sense that you've got rows and rows of small stalls, selling similar sorts of things, yet being slightly specialist. In a row of butchers one guy will be selling lamb, the next guy offal and the next man pork ... and likewise for the fishmongers. That's refreshing, because back home, more often than not, butchers will sell a whole range of meat. There's not necessarily anything wrong with that, but it's great to see people making a good living from focusing on doing one ingredient really well.

I got a nice surprise when I realized that my own cooking style fitted quite naturally with that of the Greeks. They love a lot of the same things I do, like grilled meats and fish with a little olive oil, lemon and herbs, and seriously tasty stews. Most tavernas have great big pots of home-cooked stew simmering away in the corner so the locals can eat cheaply, but well. I've got a few twists on some of their classic stews in this chapter, and they're so comforting and melt-in-the-mouth you're bound to find a new favorite among them.

Another thing I absolutely love about Greece is that it's definitely a nation that really knows how to celebrate vegetables. There are so many countries where you feel you have to work hard to get people to eat vegetables and enjoy them, but in Greece they're bloody good at getting people to embrace every type of ingredient. They have great recipes for all sorts of ingredients, be it beans, meat, greens, feta ... and, on top of that, their famous Mediterranean diet is one of the healthiest, most balanced diets in the world. But I guess that's not too surprising when you think that they've got the longest history of any Mediterranean country – they've had longer than the rest of us to get it right!

A great way to sample their culture is to hit a restaurant and order a few plates of mezze. These are similar in principle to Spanish tapas and were introduced to the country by the Turks centuries ago. They are there to be shared and picked at while you have a glass of ouzo or wine with your friends and let the world pass you by. You'll get meat dishes, little bowls of veggies or octopus, some cheese ... basically lots of different tastes, colors and textures that are delicious, fun and exciting.

When it comes to good food, good eating and feeling welcome, the Greeks really are lovely. They're a big, cuddly nation! I warmed to all the people I met on my travels, and everyone went out of their way to make sure I had a good time. If you're not being too anal and protective of what you're eating you'll be fine. Just don't go trying to turn their food into the sort of thing you'd get at your local Italian ... they'll just think, "Bloody hell! Here we go!"

After my few days in Athens I sailed out to the island of Aegina and what a change that was. Even though each island has its own vibe and style of cooking, the thing that generally pulls them together is the sheer amount of incredible fish and seafood they have access to and the light, fresh ways they prepare it.

You'll never quite get to know a city like Athens – it will always have surprises up its sleeve. But a Greek island, like Aegina, is a totally different story. In a way, I feel as though that's the real Greece. People are living as they've always done, the pace of life is slower and it's ridiculously easy to fall into their routine and let time stand still. I loved the contrast between these two worlds, and I'd definitely advise anyone to start in Athens and then venture outside the city. In a few days you can have it all: sunshine, fun, excitement, laughs and, most importantly, food!

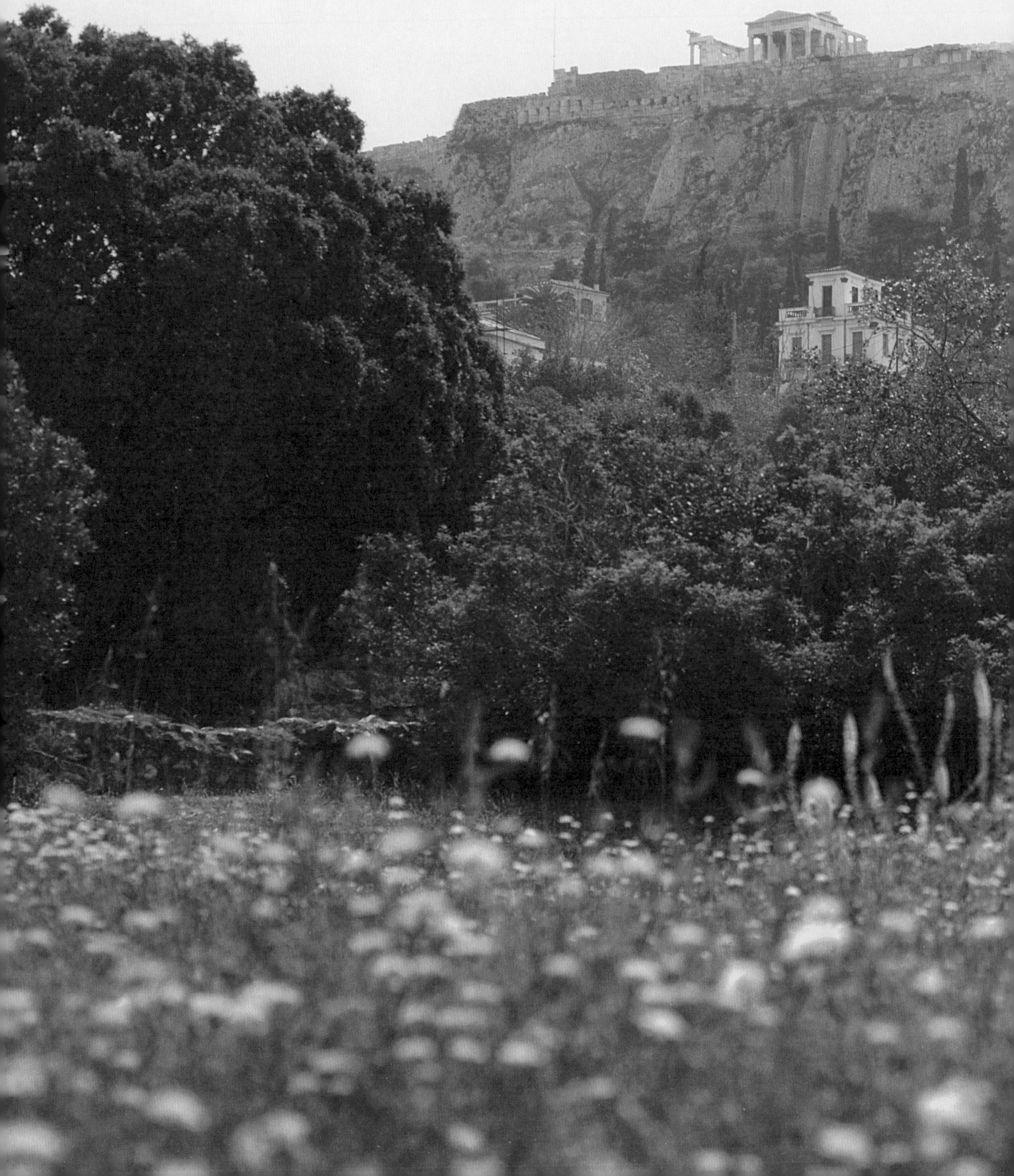

GREEK SALAD

Serves 4

- 1 medium ripe tomato
- 7 ounces ripe cherry tomatoes
- 1 beef tomato
- 1 medium red onion, peeled
- 1 cucumber
- 1 green pepper
- a handful of fresh dill
- a handful of fresh mint leaves
- a large handful of black olives, pitted
- sea salt
- 1 tablespoon red wine vinegar
- 3 tablespoons good-quality Greek extra virgin olive oil
- 7 ounce block of feta cheese
- 1 teaspoon dried oregano

This salad is known and loved around the world. Those of you who've been lucky enough to eat this salad in Greece will know that when it's made well it's absolute heaven. Hopefully this recipe will help you achieve the big bold authentic flavors that it's known for. The trick is to pay attention to the small details that make it so wonderful: things like finding the ripest tomatoes, good Greek olive oil, beautiful olives, creamy feta and lovely herbs.

I think it's quite nice to have different shapes and sizes in a salad, so cut your medium tomato into wedges, halve the cherry tomatoes and slice the beef tomato into large rounds. Put all the tomatoes into a large salad bowl. Slice the onion very finely so it's wafer thin and add to the tomatoes. Scratch a fork down the sides of the cucumber so it leaves deep grooves in the skin, then cut it into thick slices. Deseed your pepper, slice it into rings and add them to the salad along with the cucumber.

Roughly chop the dill and most of the mint leaves, reserving the smaller ones for garnish. Add the chopped herbs to the bowl of salad, then squeeze your handful of olives over so they season the vegetables, then drop them in.

Add a pinch of salt, the vinegar and the extra virgin olive oil. Quickly toss everything together with your hands. The minute all those flavors start working with the veg is when the magic starts to happen. Have a taste, and adjust the flavors if need be.

To serve, pop the block of feta right on the top of the salad. Sprinkle the oregano over the top along with the reserved mint leaves, drizzle with extra virgin olive oil and take it straight to the table. It's confident and scruffy with a bit of attitude. Delicious.

P.S. I've been known to pop leftover Greek salad into a blender with a splash of extra virgin olive oil and a few ice cubes, then blitz it up to a smooth consistency so it's basically a Greek gazpacho. It's not a classic thing to do, but it is very delicious, not to mention a great way of using up leftovers!

SIMPLE STUFFED VEG

Serves 4

- 2 large firm beefsteak tomatoes
- 2 large yellow peppers
- 2 large red peppers
- 3½ ounces shelled pistachios
- olive oil
- 2 onions, peeled and finely chopped
- 4 cloves of garlic, peeled and finely sliced
- 1 cup long-grain rice
- 1 teaspoon dried oregano
- 1 fresh red chile, deseeded and finely chopped
- sea salt and freshly ground black pepper
- 2½ cups chicken or vegetable stock, preferably organic
- 7 ounces Greek feta cheese, crumbled
- a small bunch of fresh mint, leaves picked and finely chopped
- a small bunch of fresh flat-leaf parsley, finely chopped
- 1 tablespoon tomato purée

I grew up hating the idea of stuffed vegetables – as a kid I couldn't think of anything worse! But as you can see from the picture, there's plenty of good stuff going on in this recipe, like loads of herbs and attitude. Really, the key thing here is plenty of seasoning. If you want a bit of excitement, adding chopped chile can only be a good thing. Using feta as a cooking cheese is a bit of a revelation for me. It reacts with the herbs and rice in a really interesting and delicious way. This dish is definitely substantial and bold enough to be served on its own, as a vegetarian main. Ultimately the nice thing about using peppers and tomatoes as receptacles to bake things in is that the veg add flavor to the filling and the filling adds flavor to the veg! A match made in heaven.

Preheat the oven to 400°F. Cut the tops off the tomatoes and put them to one side. Use a spoon to carefully hollow out the inside of the tomatoes. Get rid of the flesh. Halve the peppers lengthways, keeping the stalks intact. With a small sharp knife and a spoon, carefully get rid of the seeds. Place all these vegetables, cut side up, in an appropriately sized deep dish or roasting pan so that they fit quite snugly.

Toast the pistachios in a large dry pan for a few minutes, tossing occasionally, until they start to smell fantastic. Tip them into a pestle and mortar and roughly crush. Add a lug of olive oil to the pan, put it back on a low heat and, once hot, add the onions and garlic. Cook for about 10 minutes, until softened but not colored. Add the rice, oregano, chile and a good pinch of salt and pepper. Pour in 1¼ cups of stock and cook for around 7 to 10 minutes, stirring constantly, so the rice gets nicely coated in everything and doesn't stick to the pan. Remove from the heat and stir in the crumbled feta, fresh herbs and bashed-up pistachios.

Carefully stuff the hollowed-out tomatoes and peppers with your hot rice mixture so it comes just up to the top – make sure you don't overfill them, though, because the rice will expand as it cooks. Pop the tops back on the tomatoes, then drizzle over a few lugs of olive oil. Mix the tomato purée with the remaining 1¼ cups of stock and pour into the baking dish, around the veg. Cover the dish really tightly with foil and bake in the hot oven for around 1 hour and 15 minutes, or until the rice is cooked through and the vegetables are lovely and soft. Sometimes I'll whip the foil off 15 minutes before the vegetables are ready to come out. I find it helps to give the dish a bit of color and I like the way it makes the rice on top sort of crispy – but it's up to you. Remove from the oven and carefully transfer to serving plates. Serve right away while delicious and hot, with a good helping of salad and lots of beautiful crusty bread.

Souvlaki is fast food at its best. It proves that quick food doesn't have to cut corners on taste, or quality. These guys showed me the ropes, and even challenged me to a race to see if I could assemble one of these kebabs as fast as them. I didn't win, but I reckon with a bit more practice, I could!

SOUVLAKI (WICKED KEBABS)

Serves 4

(makes 8 generous kebabs)

- 3 sweet frying peppers – a mixture of colors is nice
- 8 flatbreads, to serve
- 4 sprigs of fresh mint, leaves picked
- a small bunch of fresh dill, chopped (stalks and all)
- red wine vinegar
- Greek extra virgin olive oil
- 1 lemon, to serve

For the kebabs

- 1¾ pounds boneless pork, shin if you can get it, the best quality you can afford, cut into 1 inch chunks
- 1 tablespoon dried mint
- 1 tablespoon dried oregano
- juice of 1 lemon
- 6 tablespoons good-quality olive oil
- 2 cloves of garlic, peeled and finely grated
- 1 tablespoon red wine vinegar
- a pinch of freshly ground black pepper
- a pinch of sea salt

For the tzatziki

- ½ a large cucumber
- ¾ cup plain yogurt
- 1 small clove of garlic, peeled
- 1 heaped teaspoon dried mint
- 1½ teaspoons red wine vinegar

Brits often think of kebabs as a guilty pleasure. But, having seen the love and attention that goes into preparing a proper Greek kebab, I can assure you there is nothing to feel guilty about. It's all about quality ingredients and fresh zingy flavors. I'd always thought dried mint sounded a bit odd, but actually it turned out to be very delicious and it really helped create a more authentic taste. A few of these with some cold beers would be wicked. Cook them on a grill or in a grill pan, depending on what's easier for you.

If using wooden skewers, cut 8 to fit your grill pan and soak them in a tray of water to stop them burning. Put all your kebab ingredients into a bowl and use your clean hands to mix everything together really well. Cover with plastic wrap, then pop into the fridge for 30 minutes, or longer if you want the flavors to get a bit more intense.

Meanwhile, blacken the peppers directly over a gas flame, in a hot dry grill pan or under a hot broiler. Turn them every so often and when they look almost ruined, pop them into a bowl, cover with plastic wrap and put to one side to steam for 5 minutes or so – this will help their skins to come off.

Make your tzatziki by coarsely grating the cucumber into a sieve set up over a bowl. Add a few good pinches of salt, then use your hands to squeeze out as much water as you can. Pour the water away, then tip the cucumber into the empty bowl and add the yogurt. Pound the garlic in a pestle and mortar with a good pinch of salt until you have a paste, and spoon that into the bowl with the cucumber. Add the dried mint and red wine vinegar and mix really well. Have a taste to make sure you've got the balance right, then put aside.

Preheat a grill pan or grill over high heat. Thread the skewers through the marinated pork pieces, leaving little spaces between them so that the heat cooks everything evenly. Cook the kebabs on the screaming hot pan or grill for about 8 to 10 minutes, turning occasionally until done on all sides. Warm your flatbreads in the oven or in a hot dry pan while your kebabs are cooking.

Just before your kebabs are ready, peel and deseed your blackened peppers, then tear them into strips and put them into a bowl. Roll up your mint leaves, finely slice them and add to the bowl along with the dill. Add a few splashes of red wine vinegar, a pinch or two of salt and pepper and a lug of extra virgin olive oil. Toss and mix together, then have a taste to check the balance of flavors. Cut your lemon into wedges.

Put a dollop of tzatziki and the meat from one skewer on each warmed flatbread. Top with some of your pepper mixture, a drizzle of extra virgin olive oil and a good squeeze of lemon juice. Life doesn't get much better.

MIGHTY MEATY STIFADO

This is probably one of the most famous of the Greek stews and it's definitely one of my favorites, thanks to the spices, which give it a real warmth. By marinating the meat before cooking, you get deeper layers of flavor, so that by the time the stew is ready it's like nothing you've ever tasted. Classic stifado, the kind you'll find in tavernas all over Greece, is usually made with beef, but I liked the idea of using a mixture of pork and beef so I've broken from tradition slightly with this version. Any meat, from rabbit and hare to venison, chicken or lamb, would be absolutely fantastic cooked this way.

Serves 6

- 1¼ pounds stewing beef, such as chuck or top rump, trimmed and cut into 1½ inch pieces
- 1¼ pounds trimmed pork shoulder, the best quality you can afford, cut into 1½ inch pieces
- olive oil
- 3 red onions, peeled and quartered
- 1 tablespoon raisins, roughly chopped
- 1 x 14 ounce can of chopped tomatoes
- 1 tablespoon tomato purée
- juice of ½ a lemon
- a bunch of fresh flat-leaf parsley
- Greek extra virgin olive oil

For the marinade

- 1½ teaspoons allspice berries
- 6 cloves
- sea salt and freshly ground black pepper
- 4 cloves of garlic, peeled
- 3 fresh bay leaves
- 1 cinnamon stick
- 1 teaspoon dried oregano
- ½ cup dry Greek red wine
- 4 tablespoons red wine vinegar

Bash the allspice berries, cloves and a pinch of salt in a pestle and mortar. Add the peeled garlic cloves and keep bashing until you have a paste. Tip it into a bowl, tear in the bay leaves and add the rest of the marinade ingredients. Toss the meat in the marinade until well coated, then cover with plastic wrap and put into the fridge for at least 2 hours, preferably overnight.

When you're ready to start cooking, heat a few lugs of olive oil in a large saucepan over medium heat. Add the peeled onions and cook, stirring occasionally, for 10 minutes or until softened and lightly golden. Add the meat and its marinade, then the chopped raisins, tomatoes and tomato purée, and pour in just enough water to cover everything. Season well with salt and pepper and bring everything to the boil, then reduce to a low heat, put the lid on and leave to simmer for 1½ hours. Take the lid off and cook for a further 45 minutes, or until the meat is really tender and beginning to fall apart and the sauce is thick and delicious. Keep an eye on it and add a splash of water if it looks a bit dry. Have a taste and add the lemon juice and more seasoning if necessary. Finely chop the parsley leaves and sprinkle them all over, then finish with a drizzle of good extra virgin olive oil.

Greeks serve this with rice pilaf or orzo, but it's also lovely served with hot crusty bread or mashed potatoes.

INCREDIBLE LAMB FRICASSEE MY WAY

Serves 6

- olive oil
- 2½ pounds boned leg of lamb, trimmed and cut into 1½ inch pieces
- 1 medium onion, peeled and finely sliced
- 4 cloves of garlic, peeled and finely chopped
- 2 bunches of scallions, trimmed and finely sliced
- 2 heads of romaine lettuce, washed and finely shredded
- a bunch of fresh dill, finely chopped (stalks and all)
- sea salt and freshly ground black pepper
- ¾ cup Greek yogurt

For the avgolemono sauce
- 2 large eggs, preferably free-range or organic, lightly beaten
- juice of 1½ lemons

Many people will find the idea of cooking lettuce in a stew weird, but to be honest, lettuce used to be really commonplace in soups and stews in Britain as well as in Greece. One thing's for sure, you won't regret trying this. Halfway through the cooking, the lettuce and dill won't look their best, but this stage is all about developing bold flavors, richness and making sure the meat melts in your mouth. At the next stage you'll be doing something to jazz it up so it looks beautiful and slaps you around the face with its flavors: by enriching this fricassee with avgolemono (mixed egg yolks and lemon), and just a touch of Greek yogurt, you get a thickness and a shine that really bring the flavors together to perfection. Don't miss giving this one a go.

Heat a few lugs of olive oil over medium heat in a large saucepan and add the pieces of lamb. Stir and cook for about 5 to 7 minutes, until the lamb is brown all over – you will need to do this in batches. Once done, take the meat out of the pan and add the onion, garlic and scallions. Cook for 10 minutes, stirring occasionally, until the onions begin to soften, but not color, then put the meat back into the pan.

Stir in the shredded lettuce and most of the dill and cook for a few more minutes, stirring constantly, until the lettuce has wilted. Add a few good pinches of salt and pepper and just enough water to cover the stew. Bring to the boil, then turn the heat down to a really low simmer, cover with a lid, and let it simmer for 1½ to 2 hours. After this time remove the lid and cook for a further 30 minutes, or until the lamb is beautifully cooked and pulls apart easily (nine times out of ten the lamb will be perfect after this time, but it does depend on your size of pot and the age of your lamb). Keep an eye on it as it cooks and add a splash of water if it looks like it's drying out.

When you're happy with the consistency, make the avgolemono sauce by whisking together the eggs and lemon juice until combined, then stir in an additional spoonful of Greek yogurt and a splash of water if need be. The yogurt isn't traditional, but it adds a nice creaminess I love. Your stew should be happily simmering away, so take it off the heat and very gently stir the avgolemono through it. You don't want to over-stir or the eggs will begin to set. Pop the lid on and leave for a few minutes.

Have a taste and add another pinch of salt and pepper or a squeeze of lemon juice if it needs it. Sprinkle over your reserved dill, then take the pan straight to the table so that everyone can help themselves. Serve with a tomato salad, the rest of the Greek yogurt for dolloping over, and crusty bread or mashed potatoes to mop up that delicious meaty sauce.

The Aegean Sea is bloody beautiful. We put down nets, caught an incredible variety of fish, then I jumped in the water to try my luck at spear-fishing. After that, we had more than enough fish to cook for my friends and the boat's crew. The Greek islands rock!

AEGEAN KAKAVIA (BEAUTIFUL FISH STEW)

Serves 4

- olive oil
- 2 onions, peeled and roughly chopped
- 4 sticks of celery, trimmed and roughly chopped
- 5 cloves of garlic, peeled and roughly chopped
- 3 beefsteak tomatoes, roughly chopped
- 1 pound potatoes, peeled and cut into 1–1½ inch chunks
- 3 fresh bay leaves
- 1 quart vegetable stock, preferably organic
- sea salt and freshly ground black pepper
- 1½ pounds fresh fish fillets (see above), scaled and pin-boned (sustainably caught – see introduction)
- juice of 1 lemon
- a small bunch of fresh flat-leaf parsley, roughly chopped
- a small bunch of fresh dill, roughly chopped
- Greek extra virgin olive oil
- a loaf of rustic bread, to serve

What's great about this recipe is that you can use whatever sustainably caught fish you like. Sea bass, pollack, porgy and rouget all work well. You could even use lobster if you feel like splurging! Just talk to your fishmonger and get him to recommend a few of his freshest fish. Greek fishermen make this out at sea, using whatever they've hauled into their boat that day, and cooking it in seawater. That's how I learned to make this. Because their water is ready-salted they don't need any seasoning at all to achieve a perfectly delicious stew. Genius! Try to use a mixture of fish, so you get all sorts of different flavors and colors in this wonderful stew.

Heat a good lug of olive oil in a large pan on a medium heat. Add the onions and celery and cook for 5 minutes, then add the garlic and cook for another 5 minutes, stirring occasionally, until soft but not colored.

Add the tomatoes, potatoes and bay leaves and pour in the stock. Season lovingly with salt and pepper and bring it all to the boil. Reduce to a low heat and simmer for 15 minutes. At this point, add your fish fillets and bring back to the boil, then reduce to a medium low heat and simmer for a further 15 minutes, until the potatoes are tender and the fish is cooked through and flakes apart. Stir in the lemon juice and herbs, drizzle with extra virgin olive oil, then have a quick taste to make sure you've got a good balance of acidity, freshness and seasoning and serve with chunks of rustic bread.

SHELLFISH PASTA

Serves 4-6

- olive oil
- 1 small onion, peeled and finely chopped
- 3 cloves of garlic, peeled and finely chopped
- 1 fresh red chile, deseeded and finely chopped
- ¾ pound cherry tomatoes, roughly chopped
- 18 raw, unshelled langoustines or 18 large raw shrimp, unshelled (sustainably caught – see introduction)
- ⅔ cup white wine
- 1 pound spaghetti or angel hair pasta
- sea salt and freshly ground black pepper
- zest and juice of 1 lemon, plus 1 lemon, cut into wedges, to serve
- Greek extra virgin olive oil
- a small bunch of fresh soft herbs, such as dill or flat-leaf parsley, roughly chopped

I made this on a boat on the Aegean, which was really exciting. I have to admit I was quite surprised to see pasta in Greece, but the Greeks certainly think of it as part of their culture. I definitely wouldn't want to be in the same room as a Greek and an Italian trying to figure this one out! But at the end of the day, what's a bit of flour and water between friends? This is a really quick and delicious thing to make and it showcases the amazing fresh shellfish you see all around the Greek islands. I left the shells on because that helps the langoustines stay beautiful and full of flavor as they cook. You could experiment by adding crayfish, jumbo shrimp and even mussels or clams.

Heat a couple of good lugs of olive oil in a large frying pan over medium heat and add the onion, garlic and chile. Cook for 5 minutes, stirring occasionally, until soft but not colored. Add the tomatoes, langoustines and wine, then turn the heat right up and bring everything to a fast boil. Turn down to a medium low heat and let it bubble away for 5 minutes, or until the langoustines are pink and cooked through and the sauce has reduced slightly. At this point, I quite like to grab a rolling pin and lightly crush the heads and claws of the langoustines in the pan. This helps to scent and flavor every strand of pasta you add to the pan. Sure, it might be a little messy to eat - but this is about using your hands and savoring the juices. It's a proper foodie pasta: sensual but delicious! Put a lid on the pan to keep your sauce warm.

Cook your pasta in boiling salted water according to packet instructions, until al dente. Once cooked, tip your langoustines and sauce into the pan containing the drained pasta. Add the lemon zest and juice, and a good lug of extra virgin olive oil, and season well. Toss everything together quickly, then divide between your plates and scatter over the fresh herbs. Serve with a hunk of crusty bread to mop up any juices, lemon wedges on the side for squeezing over and a glass of ice-cold ouzo.

GRILLED OCTOPUS

Serves 4

- olive oil
- a small bunch of fresh flat-leaf parsley, stalks and leaves roughly chopped
- a small bunch of fresh mint, leaves picked and roughly chopped
- 1 heaped teaspoon dried oregano
- 2 fresh red chiles, deseeded and finely chopped
- 2 fresh tomatoes, quartered
- sea salt and freshly ground black pepper
- 4 cloves of garlic, unpeeled
- 4 anchovy fillets
- 1 lemon
- 3 pound octopus, fully cleaned, all the organs removed (sustainably caught – see introduction)
- ½ a wine glass of white wine
- Greek extra virgin olive oil
- 2 tablespoons runny honey
- a small bunch of fresh thyme

Regardless of what I do to try and convince her otherwise, my wife won't let me bring octopus anywhere near her. If you feel the same way, but think of yourself as a food lover, I urge you to give this creature of the deep a try. It might look a bit dodgy, but it is delicious and exciting to eat and often really cheap to buy. By stewing then grilling it, you get incredibly tender meat on the inside and a crispy, flavorful texture on the outside. Octopus can be a bit fiddly to prepare, so get your fishmonger to do all the preparation for you so you can get straight down to the cooking. If you want to see how to do this yourself, go to www.jamieoliver.com/how-to.

By adding a few pieces of potato and other vegetables to the cooking liquor, you can create a kick-ass broth that you can pass through a sieve and store in the freezer. It will add so much flavor to all sorts of seafood dishes, from fish stews to soups. So please, if you have the opportunity to buy fresh octopus, do it – even if it scares you!

Heat 4 to 5 tablespoons of olive oil in a large casserole-type pan over medium heat. Add most of the chopped herbs and all the dried oregano to the pan with half the chopped chiles, the tomatoes and a good pinch of salt and pepper. Crush the garlic cloves with the back of a knife and add them to the pan. Stir in the anchovies, grate in the zest of your lemon, and fry for another 2 minutes over medium heat to help the flavors get going. Add the octopus, whole, and pour the wine into the pan. Pop on a lid and simmer over low to medium heat for about 30 to 45 minutes, or until the octopus is tender when pinched and you can easily insert a knife into it.

Move the octopus to a board using tongs, and take the pan off the heat. Roughly chop the octopus into bite-sized pieces and toss them in a few good lugs of extra virgin olive oil, a pinch of salt and pepper, the rest of your finely chopped chiles and the reserved chopped mint. Heat a grill pan or grill and when it's screaming hot, add your octopus pieces and grill for a few minutes until crisp and delicious.

Just before you are ready to dish up, mix a couple of spoonfuls of the cooking liquor in a bowl with the honey. Grab a small bunch of thyme and use it to brush this mixture all over the octopus as it cooks for the last 40 seconds or so. This will make it insanely delicious. This is beautiful over some fresh, lemony salad greens, with a loaf of crusty bread or on its own, with a few wedges of your zested lemon for squeezing over and your reserved chopped herbs scattered on top.

DELICIOUS DRESSED GREEK GREENS ON TOAST

Serves 4

- olive oil
- 1 small red onion, peeled and finely sliced
- ½ pound arugula or spinach, trimmed and washed
- ½ a lemon
- 2½ ounces freshly grated hard cheese, such as pecorino
- freshly ground black pepper
- 4 slices of ciabatta or sourdough bread
- 4 cherry tomatoes
- Greek extra virgin olive oil

When we pulled up to a rocky beach for an impromptu picnic I had to work with the few ingredients I had. These simple topped toasts turned out to be really delicious – the perfect snack or side dish on a hot day. Grilling the tomatoes then rubbing them over the toast adds a hint of sweetness that goes really well with the greens.

I see this as a relevant recipe for all sorts of greens, from arugula to spinach, Swiss chard or even old-school nettles. Obviously tougher greens like kale or chard will need to chug away for a bit longer, but it's all about instincts – just pay attention to what's happening in the pan and keep tasting. When they're tender and delicious they're good to go.

Get a grill pan over high heat. Put a frying pan over medium heat and add a good lug of olive oil, then add the onion and cook until soft and starting to caramelize. At this point, add your greens or spinach and leave to wilt, stirring occasionally. Squeeze in the lemon juice, then take the pan off the heat and stir in most of the grated cheese and a good pinch of pepper.

Put the slices of ciabatta and the cherry tomatoes on the hot grill pan. Turn the tomatoes and toast a few times, until nicely charred. Once done, squash a tomato on each slice of toast. Divide the greens between the toasts and scatter over the remaining cheese. Drizzle with a little extra virgin olive oil and serve immediately.

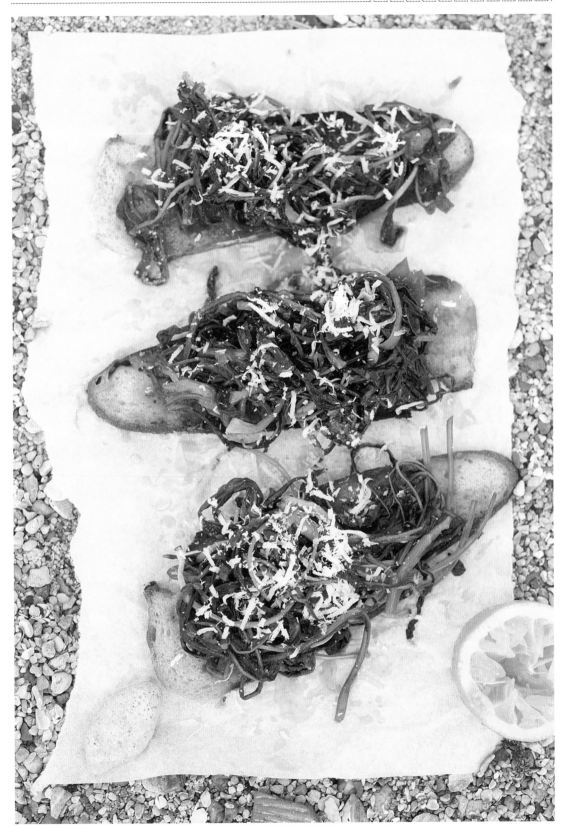

The island of Aegina is just a stone's throw away from Athens. It's one of those blessed little corners of the world where you feel lucky to be. The pace of life is slow, the people are authentic, and daily life is about finding pleasure in simple things like long, lazy lunches. They've got an ocean full of fish, grapes for wine, olives for oil, bees for honey and goats for cheese … It's its own paradise.

STICKY AND GORGEOUS PORK STEW

Serves 6

- olive oil
- 2½ pounds boned leg of pork, the best quality you can afford, trimmed and cut into 1½ inch pieces
- ½ cup good Greek red wine
- 1 tablespoon red wine vinegar
- 1 large leek, rinsed, trimmed and thickly sliced
- 2 red peppers, deseeded and roughly chopped
- 2 carrots, peeled and sliced
- 1 teaspoon dried oregano
- sea salt and freshly ground black pepper
- 1 tablespoon tomato purée
- 7 ounces prunes, pitted and roughly chopped
- juice of 1 lemon
- a small bunch of fresh flat-leaf parsley
- Greek extra virgin olive oil

Hearty exciting stews are a really big part of Greek cooking, which is why you'll find all sorts of them being served in tavernas up and down the country. My mate Andy has a friend, Nikos, who runs a lovely little restaurant in Skopelos called Agnanti. Their pork and prune stew is absolutely beautiful and after trying it I couldn't get the memory of it out of my head. I just had to do my own version. There's nothing fancy about the ingredients in this one; everything from the pork to the veg is cheap and readily available. But by giving the flavors time to mingle and adding prunes near the end, something humble is transformed into a deliciously sticky, sweet and savory dish. If you've never used prunes this way and you think it sounds strange, please try it at least once. They'll add an amazing dimension to the stew and I'm sure you'll be convinced once you taste the end result.

Heat a few lugs of olive oil in a large heavy-based pan over medium high heat. Add the pork and cook, stirring every now and then, for about 10 minutes, until the pieces start to go golden on all sides. You may need to do this in batches if your pan isn't big enough. Add the wine and red wine vinegar and cook for a further 5 minutes. Once the liquid has reduced by about two-thirds, transfer everything to a bowl and put the pan back on the heat.

Add another couple of lugs of oil to the pan, and gently fry your leeks, peppers, carrots and oregano for about 10 to 15 minutes, stirring occasionally, until softened. Tip the pork back into the pan and season to taste with a good pinch of salt and pepper. Stir in the tomato purée and enough water to just cover everything.

Bring to the boil, then turn the heat down to low, put the lid on and let everything simmer for 2 hours, until the meat is falling apart. Then add the chopped prunes and cook for another 45 minutes with the lid off, or until the pork is really tender and you've got a beautiful sticky thick sauce around it. Have a taste and add the lemon juice and a little more seasoning if necessary. Finely chop the parsley leaves and sprinkle them all over the stew. Finish the stew off with a drizzle of extra virgin olive oil, then divide between your bowls and serve next to some fluffy white rice or simple steamed greens.

GIGANTES PLAKI

Serves 6

- 1 pound dried butter beans
- olive oil
- 1 onion, peeled and finely chopped
- optional: 3 slices smoked streaky bacon, the best quality you can afford, finely chopped
- 4 cloves of garlic, peeled and finely sliced
- 2 carrots, peeled and finely sliced
- 4 large tomatoes, roughly chopped
- 1 tablespoon tomato purée
- 2 fresh bay leaves
- a small bunch of fresh flat-leaf parsley
- 1 x 14 ounce can of chopped tomatoes
- red wine vinegar
- sea salt and freshly ground black pepper
- optional: Greek extra virgin olive oil

This classic dish has loads of local variations but ultimately it's the Greek answer to baked beans! "Gigantes" means giant and "plaki" means to bake. Some recipes have fish or sausages in them (I'm using bacon in mine), so you can always dress these beans up and make them more of a main event if you like.

I've used dried beans soaked overnight, but if you're short on time you could cheat a little by using canned white beans. If you use those, just fast-forward to the second paragraph of the recipe and start there and you'll still get great results. That said, if you do have time, the slower recipe is a real goodie. I sometimes add a bouquet garni of celery, leek, thyme, rosemary, bay leaves and cherry tomatoes to the beans as they cook because it adds a nice subtle perfume. If you have those things handy, by all means add them – but if not, don't worry. The main flavor will come later when you bake the beans.

The night before you want to cook the beans, put them into a large pan, pour in enough cold water to cover them completely by a few inches, then put the lid on and leave them to soak overnight. The next day, drain the beans, put them back in the pan and cover them again with plenty of cold water. Put the pan on a high heat and, just as it comes to the boil, turn down the heat and leave the beans to simmer gently for 1 hour, or until soft and tender, skimming away any foam that rises to the top as they cook. If your beans are older they might take longer to cook, but don't worry if this happens, just make sure they're nice and tender before you stop cooking them. When ready, drain the beans in a colander and leave to one side.

Meanwhile, preheat your oven to 350°F, put a lug of olive oil into a large casserole-type pan over medium heat and gently fry the chopped onion and bacon, for about 5 minutes, or until the onions are soft but not colored. When it looks good, add the garlic and cook for a few more minutes, then add the carrots, chopped fresh tomatoes, tomato purée and bay leaves. Chop your parsley and stir it in. Add your canned tomatoes, then fill the empty can with water and add that too. Add a splash of red wine vinegar and a good pinch of salt and pepper. Give everything a good stir, and leave to simmer for 10 minutes.

Add another good pinch of salt and pepper to the pan and tip in your drained beans. Stir well, then cover the pan with a lid and cook in the hot oven for 1 hour, until the beans are really soft and a lot of the liquid has been absorbed. Have a taste and season with more salt and pepper if needed. You can serve these hot or cold (I prefer warm), with a drizzle of really good extra virgin olive oil. They'll be absolutely delicious with crumbled feta sprinkled with oregano on the side, on their own as a mezze, or with grilled fish or meat ... they're so versatile!

I don't know what makes Greek honey so delicious, but these beekeepers explained that bees are incredibly sensitive insects. Maybe they are happiest in the Mediterranean sunshine and produce the best honey there!

HONEYED FETA FILO PIES

Serves 4

- 10½ ounces feta cheese, crumbled
- 2 tablespoons Greek extra virgin olive oil, plus extra for brushing
- 4 teaspoons runny honey, plus extra to serve
- 2 teaspoons dried oregano
- 8 sheets of phyllo pastry
- 4 sprigs of fresh thyme, leaves picked
- a few teaspoons toasted sesame seeds, to serve
- olive oil

I was blown away by the contrast of textures and flavors in this gorgeous little dish from Agnanti restaurant. Even after all these years of being a chef I find there's still something really exciting about using phyllo pastry. It's quite delicate, but if you work quickly you'll be able to achieve very beautiful looks and textures. This is the sort of treat you'll find on loads of Greek street corners. With no Starbucks around (at least not yet!), getting a good coffee and one of these sweet little snacks is still the done thing. You might not think a salty cheese like feta would go well with honey, but it's a match made in heaven. It has a slight identity crisis in that it doesn't quite know if it's a dessert or a cheese course - but it's great as either. If you're torn between the two at the end of a meal, this is the perfect solution! If you'd like to see how these are made, go to www.jamieoliver.com/how-to and you'll soon be dying to give them a try.

Mix the feta, extra virgin olive oil, honey and oregano in a bowl and put aside. Lay a sheet of phyllo in front of you and brush it with a little extra virgin olive oil. Scatter over a few thyme leaves, then lay another sheet on top. Cut across the width so you've got the base for 2 parcels. Keep going until you've made 8 bases.

Divide the feta mixture into 8, then spoon one portion onto the center of each pastry base, using the back of the spoon to flatten the filling into a nice little rectangle shape. Fold in the two long sides, then fold the bottom up over the filling and then either bring the top down over that so that it forms a nice neat parcel, or wrap it up like a Christmas present - I don't mind. Toast the sesame seeds in a dry non-stick pan over medium heat for a few minutes until golden and delicious-smelling, then put to one side.

At this point you've got two choices. You can drizzle over some extra virgin olive oil, lay your parcels on an oiled baking sheet and bake them in an oven preheated to 400°F until golden and crisp. Or you can fry them. If you want to do it that way, add enough olive oil to come ¼ inch up the side of a large frying pan and put it over medium heat. Keep an eye on it and don't move the pan about too much, as hot oil is dangerous. Once the oil is nice and hot, carefully add your parcels and cook them for about 1 to 2 minutes on the folded side, until golden throughout the layers. Then flip them over and cook them for another minute, until golden brown on both sides.

Carefully remove the parcels from the oven or pan using a fish slice. Put them on paper towels to drain. Divide between 4 plates, and serve with a good drizzle of honey and a pinch or two of the toasted sesame seeds on top. Delicious as a dessert, a cheese course, or even with a lemony green salad on the side for an exciting snack.

SWEET AND LOVELY HONEY AND PISTACHIO CAKE

Serves 10-12

For the cake
- 5 large eggs, preferably free-range or organic
- 1 cup Greek yogurt
- 2 cups granulated sugar
- 4 to 5 tablespoons ground almonds
- zest of 1 lemon
- zest of 1 orange
- 1¼ cups all-purpose pan flour, plus extra for dusting
- 1 cup semolina
- 2 teaspoons baking powder
- ¾ cup plus 1 tablespoon nice mild olive oil, plus extra for greasing

For the topping
- 5 ounces shelled pistachios
- ⅔ cup good-quality runny honey

To serve
- 2 pints of strawberries, hulled and roughly chopped
- Greek yogurt

For this recipe I used beautiful pistachios from the island of Aegina and honey from a wonderful local beekeeper. Because I love the idea of embracing good local ingredients when they're available, I also decided to use some fantastic Greek olive oil in place of butter. I've used a mixture of flour and semolina, which is a bit unusual, but I think it gives the cake a really interesting texture.

Preheat your oven to 350°F. Mix all your cake ingredients in a large bowl. Grease a 9 x 11-inch cake pan with a little olive oil, then dust over a sprinkling of flour and shake the pan about. Spoon in the batter from the bowl, scraping it all out, and use a spatula to spread it evenly.

Put the cake into the hot oven to bake for about 25 to 30 minutes, until golden and cooked through. To check, remove from the oven and stick a skewer into the center of the cake. If it comes out clean it's done, so put it to one side to cool for about half an hour.

When you're just about ready to serve your cake, toast the pistachios in a dry saucepan over low to medium heat. Once they start taking on a bit of color and smelling fantastic, use a rolling pin to gently crush a few of them. Add the honey to the pan and give everything a good stir. Halve the naked orange and lemon left over from making the cake mixture and squeeze all the juice into the pan, then boil for 1 to 2 minutes, or until nice and syrupy. Don't be tempted to taste the syrup, though, as it can burn badly.

Stab the cake all over with a small knife to create holes for the syrup to sink into, then pour the pistachios and syrup all over the top and use the back of a spoon to smooth and spread it out. You want it to be fairly even so the honey gets sucked right into the cake. It will look a bit runny, but if you leave it for about 15 minutes the syrup will be soaked up. Trust me.

While it's still slightly warm, slice your cake and serve it with some chopped strawberries and a good dollop of Greek yogurt on the side. Heaven!

OCTOPUS
The Greeks love **octopus**, probably more than any other Mediterranean nation, and have countless inventive recipes and cooking techniques for it. It's very common to see octopus hanging on a line to dry before being either slowly grilled, or simply boiled whole, then chopped up and smothered in herbs. It's a cross between squid and lobster in flavor and texture.

FRESH LEMONS, SPOON SWEETS AND WILD GREENS
Lemons are used in nearly all Greek cooking, in sauces and dressings or mixed with egg to thicken stews. Fruits like cherries, figs, oranges and quince are preserved in sugar syrup to make **spoon sweets**, served as little treats to welcome guests. **Wild greens** are either picked or bought in street markets. They are used in savory pies and stews.

OLIVE OIL
Olive oil is abundant in Greece and a key element of the Mediterranean diet. Much of it is organic. New season's olive oil is called *agourelaio*, and is bright green and fruity. Greek consumption of olive oil is among the highest in the world.

FETA CHEESE

Feta, the most famous of all Greek cheeses, is made from sheep's milk, or sometimes a combination of sheep's and goat's milk. Good-quality feta is pickled in brine in wood barrels, and textures range from soft and creamy to hard and pungent. Used commonly in salads and phyllo pies, it's also found in sweet dishes.

GREEK YOGURT AND HONEY

Thick Greek **yogurt** is multi-purpose and is used for marinades, cakes, sauces, pies and savory dishes, as well as for serving next to fruit and honey. Most Greek **honey** is produced on the islands. Always used as a sweetener for pastries and desserts, or drizzled over fresh fruit and yogurt at the end of a meal.

OUZO, FRESH TOMATOES AND DRIED OREGANO

Distilled from grapes, **ouzo** is a strong, clear, aniseed-based spirit. It is flavoured with a variety of herbs and spices, such as star anise, coriander, cloves, caraway, citrus peel, fennel and mastic. The most popular accompaniment to mezze, it's served mixed with water. You'll find **tomatoes** on every Greek menu in every restaurant. They're a staple of stews, are often stuffed, and of course have a place in the world-famous Greek salad. Every household in Greece will have a bunch of dried **oregano**, which has a beautifully intense flavor because of the arid, sunny climate. Used to flavor everything from grilled meats and vegetables to stews.

FRANCE

... la 2. Truffe du Périgo...
8. T. du Gard.

FRANCE

When I was a young lad, I did a "stage" (internship) at a posh hotel in France. Even though it was very hard work, it taught me so much and really opened my eyes to what is often thought of as the greatest cuisine in the world.

Çlassic cooking techniques that I was introduced to there have never left me, and they helped to give me skills and knowledge I could take into any kitchen and apply to any type of cooking. But over the years I've fallen out of love with the linear, cheffy approach to French food you find in Michelin-starred restaurants. This time around I wanted to learn about French food from cooks, rather than chefs. It was all about cooking with mums and old boys, not a chef to be seen. So I headed to an area known as the Midi-Pyrénées in the south-west of France for a few days in the late autumn. As you can probably guess from the name, this area borders the Pyrénées mountain range, and is a place of incredible natural beauty. The Midi-Pyrénées is made up of provinces, each of which is divided into smaller "pays," or regions. Having so many communities each with its own distinct sense of identity means that every town you go to makes its own tweaks and twists to the humble dishes of the area. I'm definitely ready to fall back in love with French food.

This part of France is one of the sunniest, and although the mountains can make the weather slightly unpredictable, the overall climate is a dream come true for the farmers there. Perhaps that's why there are more working farms in the Midi-Pyrénées than anywhere else in the country. The ingredients in the local markets change blatantly with the seasons, as does the huge amount of delicious wild food in the forests. I got to taste everything from fresh and interesting salad leaves, to wild mushrooms, to wild boar and even a few delicious and highly prized black truffles, harvested in front of my eyes by a pig on her first week on the job. Throw in a glass of the dark red wine the area is famous for and life doesn't get much better.

Although the capital city of the area, Toulouse, is big and bustling, the surroundings are full of towns and small stone villages built up on rivers, lakes and mountains. It's really rural, and ridiculously pretty and quaint, as you can see from the pictures in this chapter. People have a salt of the earth quality about them and are so welcoming. I was slightly embarrassed that the kitchen French I used to speak didn't come back to me, but it didn't seem to matter. The people I met were more than happy to politely overlook that and communicate with hands and facial expressions. This trip definitely brought me back to rustic village cooking, and introduced me to some seriously tasty, unfussy dishes – the sort everyone can, and should, buy into.

Although it wasn't easy to narrow down the recipes for this chapter, these are my favorites. They reflect not only the hearty country cooking of the area, but also the ingredients this particular part of France does so well, like smoked and cured meats, beautiful cheeses and wild food. There are classic dishes like pork terrine, confit of duck and pot au feu; some kick-ass salads inspired by the fresh food I came across in the markets; and comfort food, like the zucchini gratin. And I couldn't do a chapter on French food without including a good handful of their exciting desserts, including my version of their deliciously golden sticky tarte Tatin and the pièce de résistance, crème caramel. It's true that the French like to keep what's classic, classic, so I've tried to stay true to these dishes while adding my own "local" twist here and there (OK, I'm stretching the meaning of local a bit!).

Something France really gets right is the way it fights to protect the heritage and integrity of its food products and producers. So cheeses, butter, wine and other agricultural products with a history and tradition that make them unique are protected by the AOC label (Appellation d'origine contrôlée, or "controlled term of origin"). This means that the artisan producers who make Roquefort cheese, for example, are monitored to make sure they are making their cheese in the traditional way, using the proper ingredients from a certain area and aging the cheese in the same caves at Roquefort-sur-Soulzon they've always been aged in. Only then can that cheese be called Roquefort. I love this idea because not only does it protect the quality of the food, it also means that the local traditions are safe.

STEAK TARTARE

Serves 4

- 14 ounces really good-quality beef, top or bottom round
- 2 small shallots, peeled
- 3 or 4 cornichons
- 1 teaspoon capers
- a few sprigs of fresh flat-leaf parsley
- 1 large egg yolk, preferably free-range or organic
- 1 tablespoon whole-grain mustard
- sea salt and freshly ground black pepper
- white wine vinegar
- extra virgin olive oil
- slices of toasted rustic bread, to serve

The first time I tried steak tartare I was about seventeen and working in France at a restaurant. When we went down for a staff meal one day there was an enormous pile of it on a platter for us. Everyone went crazy for it, so I figured I should give it a try, and lo and behold, it was love at first bite. Don't be put off by the fact that the meat is raw. I promise you, as long as you have really fresh, beautiful beef, this dish will be one of the tastiest things you can imagine.

The French may have claimed tartare, but there are many versions of this dish in the world. The Italians dress their beef simply with thyme tips, extra virgin olive oil and grated Parmesan, while the Lebanese use really fresh lamb, chile and mint to create a similar vibe. Manual chopping gives you multiple textures, and you can add as much or as little to it as you like. A lot of people like to use sirloin for their tartare, but really, as long as the meat is ridiculously fresh and good quality, a cheaper cut like top or bottom round will work just as well.

Finely chop and slice your beef on a big, wide wooden board until you've got very small, delicate pieces. Sweep the meat to one side of the board and finely chop your shallots, cornichons, capers and parsley in the middle of the board. Push the meat back into the center of the board, then mix and chop all those different ingredients together. Make a nest in the top of the mixture, then add the egg yolk and spoon over the mustard. Add a good pinch of salt and pepper and mix everything together.

Have a taste and really think about the seasoning. Add a good splash of vinegar and a drizzle of extra virgin olive oil (if you have new season's olive oil, this is a great way of showing it off). Mix again, then have another taste. When you're happy, serve next to a pile of hot toasted rustic bread drizzled with olive oil, and you'll have a seriously delicious starter or snack on your hands.

P.S. Once you've had a go at this great French classic, try swapping the meat for fresh venison, lamb or even buffalo if you can get it, and different herbs and flavors. Ultimately it's all about dressing beautiful meat with delicious ingredients, so just have fun with it!

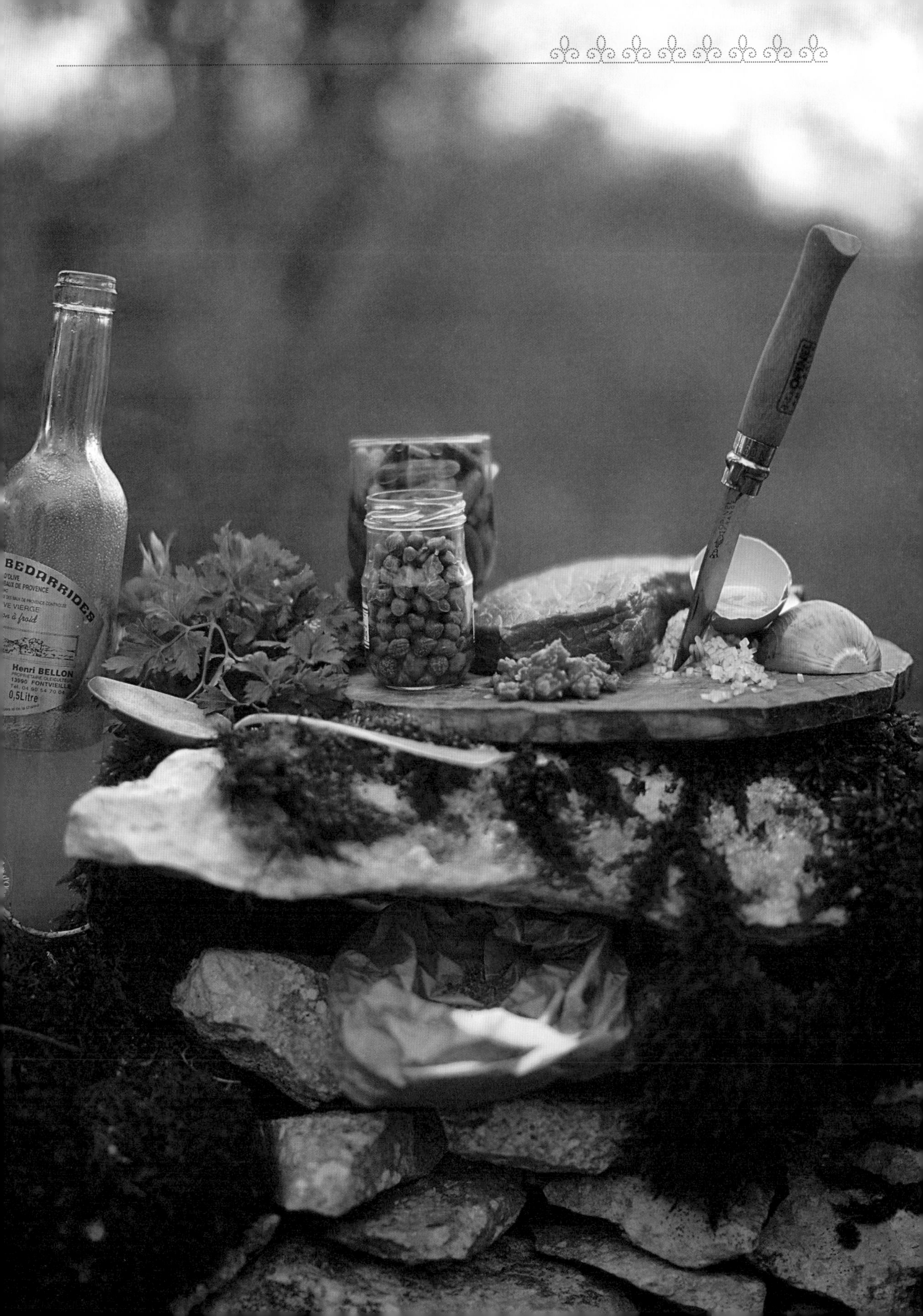
BEDARRIDES
VE VIERGE
Henri BELLON
FONTVIEILLE
0,5Litre

RADISH SALAD WITH CURED DUCK

Serves 4 as a starter

- 4 large black radishes, daikon or carrots, or a cucumber
- 9 ounces radishes - some large, some small
- 1 cured duck breast (approximately 10 ounces), thinly sliced
- rustic country bread, to serve

For the dressing

- a very small bunch of fresh flat-leaf parsley, finely chopped, stalks and all
- 2 shallots or ½ a small red onion, peeled and finely grated
- 2 tablespoons red wine vinegar
- 6 tablespoons extra virgin olive oil
- sea salt and freshly ground black pepper

I found the most incredible varieties of radishes at the farmers' market in Cahors: big, small, red, black ... they were beautiful. If you pay a little attention to preparing them, by chopping the bigger ones up so that they are quite chunky, slicing the medium ones into delicate thin rounds and halving the tiny ones or leaving them whole, you'll end up with a fresh salad with lots of interesting textures and colors.

The charcuterie in town stocked some beautiful cured duck, which I've used here. It can be hard to find - you'll need to look in speciality stores or online. Don't let that stop you enjoying this salad, though, because bresaola or other rich cured game will work just as well. Ultimately what I love about this salad is the contrast of flavors: the smooth rich texture of the duck, with the juicy crunch and peppery goodness of the radishes.

Wash and scrub all your radishes. If you're using carrots, peel them and slice them into rounds. If you're using cucumber, halve it lengthways, scoop out the watery seeds, then slice. If you managed to find black radishes, peel away most of the thicker skin, then slice them into rounds and put them into a bowl. Halve the smaller radishes, leaving any tiny ones whole, then cut up the large and medium radishes into uneven slices to give some variety and add to the bowl.

Put the chopped parsley, grated shallots, red wine vinegar and extra virgin olive oil into a jam jar or small bowl. Season with a good pinch of salt and pepper, then mix and have a taste. Adjust with a splash more vinegar or seasoning if needed. Add the slices of cured duck to the bowl of radishes, then drizzle your dressing all over the salad and quickly toss and dress with your clean hands.

Serve right away, with a hunk of warm rustic bread, while the radishes are as crunchy and delicious as possible.

PORK TERRINE

Serves 10-12

- 3⅓ pounds pork – a mixture of neck, shoulder and a tiny bit of leg, the best quality you can afford, coarsely ground
- 3½ ounces pork or chicken liver, the best quality you can afford
- 3½ ounces bacon, the best quality you can afford, chopped
- a small bunch of fresh thyme, leaves picked
- a bunch of fresh flat-leaf parsley, finely chopped (stalks and all)
- ½ teaspoon ground cloves
- 1 whole nutmeg, for grating
- 3 or 4 small fresh bay leaves
- a large handful of good-quality breadcrumbs
- 1 level teaspoon white pepper
- sea salt

Unless you're buying a terrine from a truly amazing artisan producer you really won't get any better than one you've made yourself. I haven't used a traditional terrine mold here (which is where the recipe gets its name) because most people tend to have flat round dishes at home. Basically as long as you make this in an ovenproof dish that's 2 inches deep, it will cook in the same time as I'm giving you here.

Keeping a mix of textures and colors from the different cuts of meat will make this delicious and interesting to eat. You can ask your butcher to grind your pork for you, or pulse it in a food processor, slicing and finely chopping a few bits to give you a great mixture of little lumps, chunks and fine bits. If you leave the terrine in the dish you cooked it in, with all the fat around the edge, and make sure it's properly covered, it will keep happily in the fridge for up to a week.

About 20 minutes before you're ready to start cooking, take the meat out of the fridge so it can come up to room temperature. Preheat your oven to 325°F. Blitz the liver and bacon to a purée in a food processor, then tip into a large bowl with the ground pork mixture. Add the thyme, parsley and ground cloves, then grate in half your nutmeg. Roll your bay leaves up like a cigar and finely chop them, then add to the bowl with the breadcrumbs, white pepper and 3 really good pinches of salt.

Get your clean hands in there and scrunch everything up until really well mixed. If you can, I recommend you use a round earthenware dish here as it will work with these timings – you need one approximately 10 inches in diameter and 2 inches deep. Overfill the dish first, then really push and squash the mixture down and right out to the edges.

Place the dish in a large roasting pan and create a bain-marie by half-filling the roasting pan with hot water. Put this into the oven and leave to cook slowly for 1 hour and 15 minutes. You can check it's done by inserting a knife into the center – if the juices run clear it's perfect. It will have shrunk a bit during cooking but that is perfectly normal so don't be alarmed. Remove from the oven and leave in the bain-marie to cool. Don't be tempted to drain off any of the juices, because once the terrine cools they will help to keep it moist. Once cool, cover the terrine with plastic wrap and chill in the fridge until ready to eat.

I like to put the terrine in the middle of the table, then serve it in wedges with a salad of cornichons, radishes and endive, dressed with red wine vinegar and extra virgin olive oil. Just remember to think about contrast, texture and flavor when you're deciding what to serve it with. Add a dollop of mustard and some slices of hot toast, with a lovely glass of French Malbec wine on the side, and you're talking.

I love the fact that even the smallest of villages still has an epic weekly market, where not only are you guaranteed to find great in-season produce, you're also sure to find local producers specializing in doing one thing really well, whether it's pastries, cheese or charcuterie. There's no better way to show your support for what they do than shopping this way.

MARKET SALAD WITH WALNUTS AND RUSTIC GOAT'S CHEESE CROUTONS

Serves 4

- 4 large handfuls of lamb's lettuce (mâche)
- inner leaves from 1 frisée lettuce
- 1 small yellow endive, broken into leaves
- 1 bunch of radishes
- a loaf of sourdough bread
- a large handful of shelled walnuts
- 5 ounces soft goat's cheese

For the dressing

- 2 small shallots, peeled and very finely sliced
- 4 tablespoons walnut oil
- 2 tablespoons extra virgin olive oil
- 2 or 3 tablespoons red wine vinegar
- a few sprigs of fresh flat-leaf parsley, finely chopped
- a good pinch of sea salt and freshly ground black pepper

This salad is simplicity itself and I love it. All these ingredients came from the local market, but you can use any interesting, bouncy salad leaves and crunchy vegetable you like. It might seem wasteful, but the outer green leaves of the frisée lettuce can be quite bitter. Click those off and use the fresh yellow leaves for your salad.

Serve it next to these uneven toasts or break the toasts up over the top like croutons. This makes a great lunch or starter. Since coming back from this trip I've made it for my kids and served it with leftover meats. They love it.

Preheat a grill pan. Wash all your salad leaves, spin them dry, and tip them into a large bowl. Finely slice the radishes, leaving any smaller ones whole, and add them to the bowl too.

Mix your dressing ingredients in a jam jar, then have a taste and check the seasoning, adding another little swig of vinegar or a pinch of salt if it needs it. Put to one side.

Slice the bread lengthways so you've got 8 long thin slices. Toast them on the hot dry grill pan, turning them over every few minutes until they have lovely char marks on both sides (or pop them in a hot oven if that is easier). While they toast, slice the walnuts as thinly as you can and sprinkle them over the salad.

Once the toast is done to your liking, take it off the heat and snap the slices into uneven pieces. Smear each one with goat's cheese, then quickly toss and dress your salad and bang it in the middle of the table, with the croutons spread out around it or on top so everyone can help themselves.

THE MOST BEAUTIFUL WARM QUAIL SALAD

**Serves 4 as a main or
8 as a starter**

- olive oil
- 4 quail
- sea salt and freshly ground
  black pepper
- 4 thick slices of rustic bread
- a few sprigs of fresh
  rosemary, leaves picked
- 2 cloves of garlic, unpeeled
- 4 slices of bacon, the best
  quality you can afford
- 2 large handfuls of red or
  mixed seedless grapes
- red wine vinegar
- extra virgin olive oil
- a few handfuls of lamb's
  lettuce (mâche), washed and
  spun dry
- a few handfuls of inner
  leaves from 1 frisée lettuce,
  washed and spun dry
- a few handfuls of watercress,
  washed and spun dry
- 1 red endive or radicchio,
  washed and finely sliced

Wherever I go in the world I love making warm salads - there's something about taking exciting leaves and dressing them at the very last minute with a pan-fried or roasted element that I just can't resist. As with any warm salad, the key is getting hungry people around the table and ready to eat because warm salads are only at their best just after they're made. I'm using quail, but a poussin chicken, wood pigeon, or even a few duck legs from the confit on page 324 would give you equally delicious results. I love the fact that the birds cook at the same time as your croutons, allowing them to suck up as much flavor as possible. I've even made my dressing right in the sheet, using all the sticky goodness you'd normally scrub off the bottom, so you get maximum flavor, and minimum washing up!

Preheat your oven to 350°F. Drizzle olive oil over each quail and season them well with salt and pepper, rubbing it into the birds.

Roughly tear the slices of bread into 1-inch pieces and scatter these around the base of a large roasting pan, along with the rosemary leaves. Crush the garlic cloves with the back of a knife and add them to the pan, then drizzle over some olive oil and lay the quails on top of the croutons. Drape and fold a bacon slice across the breast of each bird. Put the pan into the hot oven and roast for to 35 to 40 minutes, or until the bacon is crisp and golden and the quails are cooked through (give one of the legs a gentle tug - if it pulls away easily and the meat shreds apart they're done).

Take the tray out of the oven and carefully move each quail to a board. Use a large knife to quickly and confidently cut them in half lengthways. Return them to the pan and push everything to one half of the pan. Pick out the garlic cloves and squeeze their soft flesh into the juices in the pan, and get rid of the skins. Rest the half of the pan with all the croutons etc. on a board so the cooking juices pool down at the bottom.

Take the grapes in your clean hands and really scrunch and crush them up into the juices in the empty half of the pan. Rub and mix the grapes with the juices, unsticking as much goodness from the bottom of the pan as you can. Season with a really generous pinch of salt and pepper, and add a good splash of red wine vinegar and a lug of extra virgin olive oil. Have a taste and adjust if you think it needs more acid or seasoning. Get everyone around the table, then lay your salad leaves on top of the warm dressing and quickly but delicately toss them, pulling in the quail halves and croutons as you go. Move everything to a large platter or, if the roasting pan is nice looking, take it straight to the table with a pair of tongs and serve right away.

P.S. The timings here are great for quail, but it may take slightly more time to cook a poussin, so bear that in mind if you use that instead.

ROQUEFORT SALAD WITH WARM CROUTONS AND LARDONS

Serves 4 as a main

- olive oil
- 8 ounce piece of smoked streaky bacon, the best quality you can afford, rind removed
- 2 thick slices of sourdough bread, cut into ½ inch pieces
- 4 large handfuls of lamb's lettuce (mâche), watercress or rocket, washed and spun dry
- 2 large handfuls of radicchio, washed and spun dry
- a large handful of shelled walnut halves, sliced
- a bunch of fresh chives, finely chopped
- Roquefort cheese

For the dressing

- 6 tablespoons extra virgin olive oil
- 2 tablespoons red wine vinegar
- 1 tablespoon Dijon mustard
- sea salt and freshly ground black pepper

Roquefort is a fantastic cheese, with a great story behind it. A few hundred years ago there was a guy out in the forest eating some cheese, when a foxy chick walked past. Not wanting to miss out, he threw his cheese into a cave to keep it safe and ran after the girl. He returned a few weeks later to retrieve his cheese and found it had gone moldy, but in a good way, and had really matured. Ever since then, proper authentic Roquefort has to be aged in those same stone caves of Mont Combalou at Roquefort-sur-Soulzon. Genius!

This salad really shows off the Roquefort, and several other great French ingredients, most of which can be found without any trouble. It's worth getting bacon from the butcher so you have lovely extra-large hand-cut lardons for this. The kick-ass mustard dressing adds a bit of flair at the end, and ultimately, this salad is my homage to my dear French friends and that lucky man from all those years ago who invented such a great cheese and hopefully had one of the best hook-ups of his life!

Put a large frying pan on a high heat, and once hot, add a good couple of lugs of olive oil. Cut your bacon into half-inch lardons (have a look at the picture – that's roughly the size your croutons and bacon should be), and add to the pan. Fry, stirring occasionally, for around 3 minutes, or until you've got a good bit of color on the bacon and a lot of the fat has rendered out. Turn the heat down a little and add your bread to the pan, making sure you spread the croutons out so they take on some color. Fry for another 3 minutes, or until they've sucked up all the wonderful flavor and are lovely, crisp and golden.

Put the extra virgin olive oil, red wine vinegar, Dijon mustard and a good pinch of salt and pepper into a clean jam jar. Put the lid on and give it a shake, then have a taste and make sure you've got the balance right. You want it to be slightly too acidic at this stage, as you'll get quite a bit of saltiness from the bacon and French dressings tend to be quite sharp.

Once your dressing is made, get everyone around the table so they're ready to tuck in as soon as the salad is ready. Put your salad leaves on a big platter, tear in the radicchio, then pour over that wonderful, thick dressing. Scatter over most of your walnuts and chives and all the croutons and lardons. Quickly mix it all up with your clean hands so that every single leaf is coated.

Use the tip of a knife to crumble off little nuggets of Roquefort and let them fall straight on to your salad. Finish by scattering over the rest of the walnuts and chives from a height, and tuck in!

It's not every day you get the chance to go truffle hunting with a man and his pig, so I really made the most of this pretty unusual afternoon. It was the pig's first week on the job. She was good, and even though she was a bit crazy and all over the place, she managed to dig up some lovely black truffles. I love the fact that an ingredient so prized in the restaurant industry grows wild and is there for anyone, rich or poor, to discover and make the most of (or sell!).

THE KING OF OMELETTES
(BLACK TRUFFLE OMELETTE)

Serves 1

- olive oil
- 3 large eggs, preferably free-range or organic
- a pinch of sea salt
- a touch of white pepper
- 1 small fresh black truffle
- a knob of butter

On this trip I saw a lady make an omelette in the simplest, but coolest way. You may think that sounds crazy, but honestly, it's changed the way I'm making omelettes at the moment. Instead of beating the eggs, she sort of ran her fork through them in the bowl so they were only just broken. The omelette she ended up with was marbled, and had amazing texture, because of the way she knotted and twisted the eggs as they cooked ... so pretty! There's a video for you on www.jamieoliver.com/how-to if you want to see this being made. This technique will work beautifully with ham, cheese, mushrooms or any other flavor you fancy.

I decided to try her method out with one of the most prized ingredients in the whole world: black truffles. They are definitely one of those ingredients that are alluring and mysterious. If you haven't ever had fresh truffle, I can promise you it's an experience worth waiting for. This recipe is a great way to showcase truffles, because silky eggs and shavings of truffle are best friends.

Put a non-stick frying pan (approximately 8 inches) over fairly high heat and drizzle in a little olive oil. While it's getting nice and hot, crack the eggs into a bowl and add the salt and white pepper. Using a small sharp knife, shave a few fairly thick slivers of truffle into the bowl. Now, although you would normally really whip this up, I'm going to use my new technique: just run a fork through the eggs, then sort of fold them together, breaking up the yolks a little, so they're lightly marbled.

Add a knob of butter to the pan and, once melted, pour the eggs into the pan. Be confident and work quickly. Count to 5, then pull the cooked egg away from the bottom and sides of your pan with a spatula or spoon. Count to 5 again and do that one more time. When the uncooked egg on top is just starting to set, get a spatula and flip the top over. Put a large serving plate over the pan and quickly and confidently turn it out. Serve straight away, next to a few hunks of rustic bread and a glass of wine if you're having a relaxed light lunch.

P.S. If you do get your hands on a fresh truffle and don't want to put it into an omelette, this tip is perfect for you. Pop a few eggs into an airtight container and place the truffle on top. Leave it in there for a few days and the aroma and flavor of the truffle will penetrate the porous eggshells and you'll be able to have scrambled or boiled eggs that taste of truffle in the most wonderful, subtle way.

SAVORY CHESTNUT CRÊPES

Makes 4-6 crêpes

- 1 large egg, preferably free-range or organic
- 1 regular coffee mug full of chestnut flour
- 1 regular coffee mug full of whole milk
- sea salt and freshly ground black pepper
- olive oil
- a few sprigs of fresh rosemary, leaves picked
- 4-6 slices of lovely ham or prosciutto
- Gruyère cheese, for grating

A savory crêpe is always wonderful, but the minute you swap regular flour for chestnut flour and add some lovely cured meat and cheese to the equation, things start to feel a bit special. Chestnut flour is a really exciting ingredient. It's got a very fine texture and is naturally sweet, so it suits being made into dessert crêpes and served with chocolate, ice cream or fruit. Personally I think it makes for an exciting savory crêpe – you just have to push the seasoning to convince the batter it is savory. These are a little more rustic than your average crêpe, so don't worry about them looking too pretty, it's all about knocking out really thin, but rough-and-ready delicious crêpes and serving them while they're lovely and hot. You should be able to track down chestnut flour in most good supermarkets, but if not, see the P.S. at the bottom of this recipe.

Crack the egg into a bowl and add the chestnut flour, milk and a really good pinch of salt and pepper. Whisk together until you have a smooth batter. Put a spoon in the mixture to check the consistency. You want it quite runny, so add another splash of milk if you think it's too thick, then put to one side.

Preheat a medium non-stick pan over medium heat and let it get good and hot. Drizzle in a little olive oil, then add a pinch of rosemary leaves. Tear one of your slices of prosciutto into small pieces and add these to the pan. Keep everything moving around for a minute or until crisp. Try to spread your rosemary and ham around the pan so it's quite evenly spaced, then ladle in enough batter to thinly coat the base of the pan. Cook until it's starting to set around the edges, and finely grate over a thin layer of Gruyère.

As soon as the crêpe is golden and lovely underneath, get an offset spatula and fold it over in half. Grate over a little more Gruyère, then flip the crêpe over and do the same over that half. Cook for another minute or so, turning as you go, until you have a delicious, golden and crisp crêpe. Repeat until you've used up all your ingredients, then serve as part of a light lunch, with a fresh green salad and a glass of wine.

P.S. To make your own chestnut flour, blitz 3½ ounces of **vacuum-packed chestnuts** to a fine powder in a food processor. Add 1 regular coffee mug full of **milk**, 1 **egg** and a really good pinch of **salt and pepper**. Biltz again, then mix in ¾ cup of **all-purpose flour** until you have a smooth batter. If you want to roughly pulse in some more chestnuts at this point for a bit of texture, that would also be lovely.

Croustilot

BATIMENTS DE FRANCE

4129 SV 28

These outfits might look kind of strange, but I love what they represent: pride and respect for great food and cooking traditions. These guys are the Brotherhood of the Croustilot and they are named for the fantastic artisan bread their organization has been making for centuries. It goes without saying that they take their bread very seriously and I don't blame them.

COUNTRY CHICKEN AND BEAN SOUP

Serves 6-8

- 9 ounces dried navy beans
- olive oil
- 4 slices of bacon, the best quality you can afford, finely sliced
- 3 onions, peeled and very finely sliced
- 5 cloves of garlic, peeled and finely sliced
- 1 whole chicken (approximately 2½ pounds), preferably free-range or organic
- sea salt and freshly ground black pepper
- 1 fresh bay leaf
- a small bunch of fresh thyme
- a small bunch of fresh flat-leaf parsley
- ½ a Savoy cabbage
- 4 carrots, peeled and finely sliced
- a loaf of rustic bread, to serve

It's no great surprise that, come autumn, the area of France that borders the Pyrénées starts to favor ingredients like cabbage and beans ... they are some of the only things available. When they are used in a fantastic soup like this, you'll get a hearty, filling meal that tastes fresh, clean and delicious.

For me, this soup is all about the incredible flavor the chicken bones will add, although if you wanted to, you could use a chunk of bacon or a few chicken wings instead. Ultimately you're looking to bring out the flavor of the simple ingredients and jazz the whole thing up by creating a wicked broth. If you wanted to stir through a handful of nice melty cheese, like Gruyère, at the last minute, that would be really delicious too.

The night before you want to make your soup, put the dried beans into a large pan or bucket and cover them with cold water. Pop the lid on and leave them to soak overnight to soften and rehydrate.

The next day, put a really large deep pot over medium heat and, once hot, add a good lug of olive oil and the sliced bacon. Fry for around 5 minutes, or until the bacon starts to get a little color. Tip in the sliced onions and garlic and cook slowly for 20 minutes, stirring frequently, or until you have a soft, lightly golden, sticky mixture.

Place the chicken on top of the onion mixture, then drain the beans and add them to the pot. Pour in enough cold water to just cover everything and season with a good pinch of salt and pepper. Make a kind of bouquet garni by tying the bay, thyme and parsley together with string, and add to the pot. Bring to the boil, skimming away any foam that rises to the top, then reduce to a gentle simmer and pop the lid on. Leave it to simmer for 1 hour, checking occasionally and skimming away any more foam that comes to the surface.

Meanwhile, get rid of the outer leaves of your cabbage. Peel off the lush dark green leaves, leaving the heart intact. Give the leaves and the heart a good wash, then roll the outer leaves up like a cigar and finely slice them, along with the heart.

Check your chicken is cooked by gently tugging at a leg - if it comes away easily and the meat pulls apart, it's done. Use tongs to carefully remove the chicken and herbs to a board. Add the sliced cabbage and carrots to the pot and cook over high heat with the lid off for 30 minutes, or until your vegetables are tender and cooked through. Use forks to shred the chicken meat off the bones and get rid of the skin, any bones and the bouquet garni. At this point, you can either keep the shredded chicken for amazing sandwiches or stir it back into the soup (I like to do a bit of both). When the cabbage and carrots are ready, have a taste and season with salt and pepper. Serve with some hunks of rustic bread. Heaven in a bowl.

ZUCCHINI GRATIN

Serves 6-8 as a side

- 2 tablespoons duck fat (or olive oil if you prefer)
- 3 onions, peeled and very finely sliced
- 1 cup basmati rice
- 7 medium zucchini, finely sliced
- 2 cups hot chicken or vegetable stock, preferably organic
- 4 heaped tablespoons crème fraîche
- 5 ounces Emmental or Cheddar cheese, finely grated
- sea salt and freshly ground black pepper
- olive oil

This recipe was inspired by a simple country dish I saw being made by the lovely Monique, the owner and cook of a little restaurant called Lou Bourdie in the village of Bach. It's not obviously French, but flavor-wise it really conjures up the whole mentality of food in this area: incredibly simple, yet delicious. I was bowled over by it, and I hope you will be too. The secret of making it a success is to use the best stock you can get your hands on. Monique was using the broth from a big pot au feu, which was bubbling away on the stove, for hers, and I'm sure that added all sorts of wonderful flavors (see page 316). I've used a combination of crème fraîche and Emmental, so it's gooey in some places, crispy in others.

Preheat the oven to 375°F. Get a large frying pan on a low heat and add the duck fat (or you could use olive oil here if cooking for veggies) and a splash of water. Once melted and hot, add the sliced onions and cook for 20 minutes, stirring occasionally, or until soft and sticky. Meanwhile, rinse your rice under cold running water until the water runs clear.

When the onions look ready, add the sliced zucchini to the pan along with the rice. Mix them up, then pour in the hot stock. Turn the heat up and cook for 5 minutes, stirring occasionally. You want the mixture to stay quite loose and oozy, so add a little more stock if needed. Take the pan off the heat and gently stir in the crème fraîche and 3½ ounces of your grated cheese. Add a good pinch of salt and pepper, then have a taste and adjust the seasoning if need be.

Lightly oil a roasting pan, gratin dish or casserole-type pan, approximately 10 x 12 inches. Tip everything into your prepared pan, making sure the rice is evenly distributed. Roughly flatten it out and try to get most of the zucchini on top to help keep in the moisture as it cooks. Sprinkle over the rest of the grated cheese.

Bake in the hot oven for 40 minutes, or until the top is golden and bubbling and the rice is beautifully cooked and has absorbed most of the liquid. Serve next to grilled meat or fish and a lovely fresh salad.

POT AU FEU

Serves 4

(with lots of meat left over)

- 1 x 2 pound piece of beef shin or brisket
- 1 x 14 ounce piece of pork belly, the best quality you can afford, rind removed
- 2 onions, peeled and halved
- 1 teaspoon peppercorns
- 4–5 cloves of garlic, peeled
- sea salt and freshly ground black pepper
- 1 whole chicken (approximately 3⅓ pounds), preferably free-range or organic
- 10½ ounces Toulouse-style French sausage
- 4 medium potatoes, peeled and halved
- 2 long turnips, peeled, or 4 baby turnips, peeled and halved
- 1 small rutabaga (approximately 1 pound), peeled and roughly chopped
- 4 carrots, peeled
- rustic bread, to serve
- Dijon mustard, to serve

For the bouquet garni

- 1 stick of celery, with leaves
- 2 fresh bay leaves
- a small bunch of fresh thyme
- a small bunch of fresh flat-leaf parsley
- optional: a couple of outer leaves from 1 leek

This is a proper French classic with simple clean flavors, and trust me: it tastes damn good. I think of it as a few simple steps to great family or party food. It's about gathering and building flavor as you go, and you can vary what you use to suit the season. Mine's quite autumnal, but you could add peas, asparagus, candy-colored beets or a handful of spinach to freshen things up in the sunnier months.

All I will say is that if you're going to make this, just make it properly and get the largest, tallest pot you can lay your hands on. This recipe makes a great meal for four people, but there's enough meat to do you another couple of meals as well. You can use the leftovers in sandwiches, pies or terrines – so don't go worrying about eating all the meat in one sitting, that would be bonkers! If you have any leftover broth, use it for stock or soup.

This recipe has a lot going on ingredients-wise, so you need to use a really big pot. It sounds obvious, but make sure you've got one large enough to hold everything before you start.

Put your beef shin or brisket and pork belly into the pot and add the onions, peppercorns, garlic and a really good pinch of salt and pepper. Make a kind of bouquet garni by wrapping all the ingredients in the outer leaves of a leek and tying it up with string. If you don't have a leek, simply tie all your herbs together. Add this to the pan with enough cold water to just cover everything.

Place on a high heat and bring to the boil, skimming off any foam that rises to the surface. Once boiling, immediately reduce the heat to a steady simmer and cook for 1½ hours with the lid on, checking occasionally and skimming away any further foam. Keep an eye on the water level as it cooks, and top up with a little more water if needed.

Add your chicken and Toulouse sausage to the pot, using tongs to help you rearrange everything so that the chicken is completely submerged (add a splash more water if needed). Simmer for 30 minutes, then add your potatoes, turnips, rutabaga and carrots and simmer for another hour.

Traditionally, the meat would be removed to a board, the veg to a platter, and the broth would be served as a soup to start, followed by a plate of meat and veg. But you can also transfer all the meat to a board using tongs and carve, then divide the veg between your bowls, add some meat and ladle over the broth. Serve with rustic bread and a good dollop of Dijon mustard. Store the leftover meat, veg and broth in the fridge and use them up within 2 or 3 days.

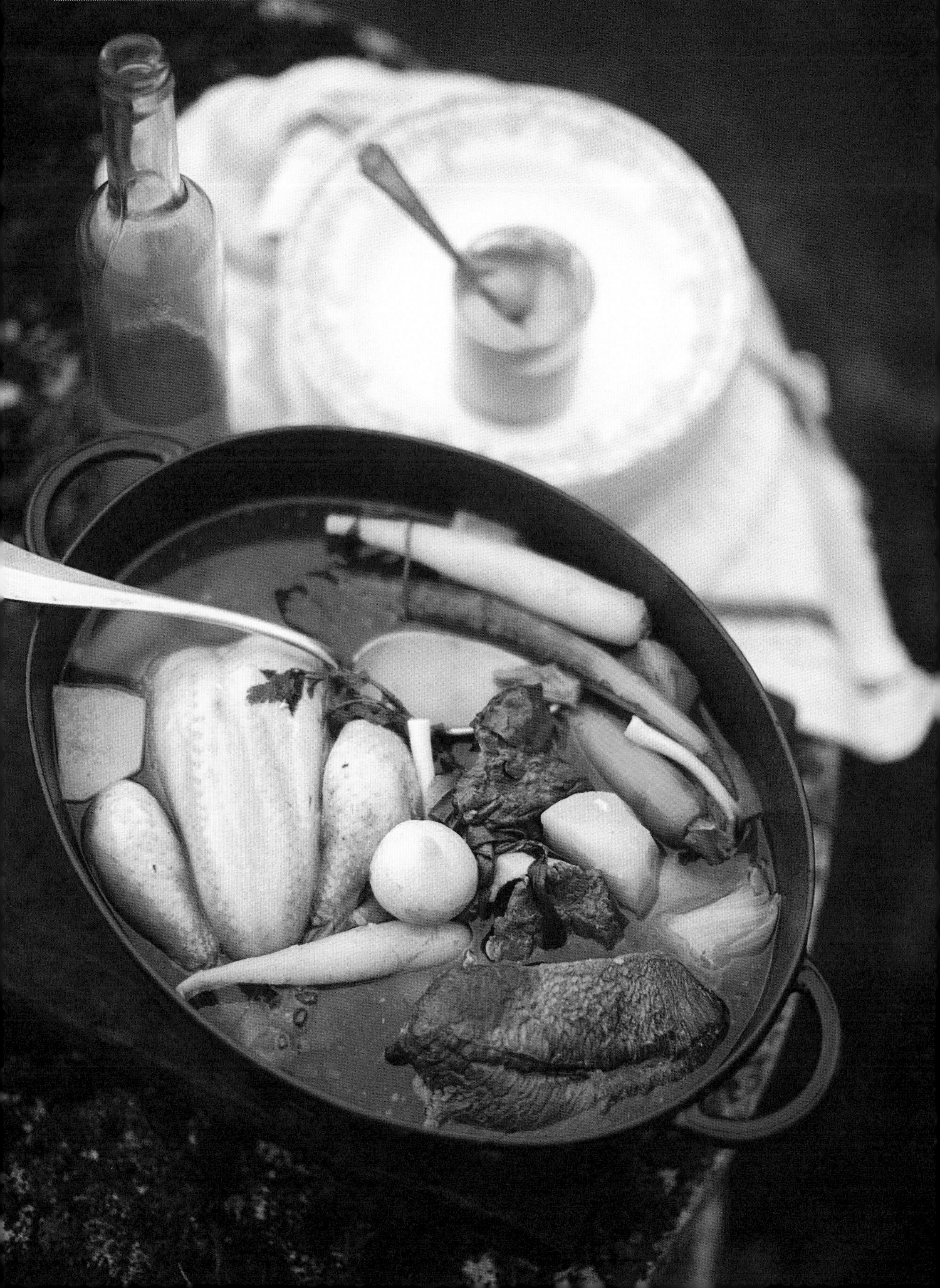

ROAST LAMB WITH BEANS

Serves 6

- 1 x leg of lamb (approximately 4½ pounds), on the bone
- sea salt and freshly ground black pepper
- olive oil
- 10 cloves of garlic, peeled
- a small bunch of fresh thyme
- a couple of sprigs of fresh rosemary
- 3 medium leeks, peeled and sliced diagonally 1 inch thick
- 2 onions, peeled and finely sliced
- 1 fresh bay leaf
- 2 small bunches of fresh flat-leaf parsley
- 4 x 14 ounce cans of flageolet beans
- 6⅓ cups lamb, chicken or vegetable stock, preferably organic

I love the hearty, incredible flavors you get with this dish. By roasting the lamb on a rack directly over the beans, you make sure none of the gorgeous juices that cook out of the lamb go to waste. I used flageolet beans in France because they are very popular there, but really any good-quality canned or jarred white beans, like navy or butter beans, would be delicious.

When it comes to cooking the lamb you've got two choices: slow-roasting or roasting. When I made this in France I slow-roasted a leg of lamb then shredded it apart on top of the beans (as you can see from this picture). However, there's also something beautiful about roasting a leg, slicing it up and serving it slightly blushing – so I've decided to give you both options in this recipe.

Preheat the oven as high as it will go and get your lamb out of the fridge. Stab it all over with a small sharp knife, then rub all over with a good pinch of salt and pepper and a lug of olive oil. Slice 4 garlic cloves and poke the slices into the incisions you've made, along with some small sprigs of thyme and rosemary. Put the leeks, onions and 6 cloves of garlic into a deep roasting pan. Add a good lug of olive oil and a pinch of salt and pepper, then put on a medium heat and cook, stirring occasionally, for 15 minutes, or until the leeks and onions have softened.

Make a kind of bouquet garni by tying the bay, the rest of the thyme and one of the bunches of parsley together with string. Add that to the pan along with the canned beans and their juices. Pour in all the stock and give everything a good stir.

Place your lamb directly on an oven rack, with the pan of beans on the shelf below it. If you want blushing meat, immediately turn the oven down to 350°F and cook for 1¼ hours. Let the leg rest for 15 minutes on a board, covered with foil, and you'll end up with beautifully pink meat that is perfect for carving. Your beans will still be quite liquidy at this point, so put them over a high heat and let them cook and reduce down while your lamb rests.

If you want sticky pull-apart meat, turn the oven down to 325°F immediately after the lamb goes in and cook your lamb and beans for about 3 hours, or until the meat shreds apart easily. Move the leg to a board, cover with foil and leave to rest for 30 minutes. Cover the beans with foil, turn the oven off and leave them in there to keep warm until serving.

When ready to serve, take your beans out of the oven and spoon a third of them into a bowl. Use a potato masher to mush them up, then stir them back through the rest of the beans to make them really lovely and creamy. Finely chop your remaining bunch of parsley and stir this through the beans. Slice or shred your lamb, then serve it over those gorgeous beans and tuck in.

When I set off on a boar hunt with this group of Frenchmen
I really hoped the basic French I once spoke all those years
ago would come back to me. Embarrassingly, it didn't, but
somehow we muddled through and we had a great time over
a long supper back at the lodge and plenty of eau de vie! I
guess when your love for their good food, good wine and good
company comes across, they can see that and you're all right

GORGEOUS ROSEMARY PRUNE SKEWERS

Makes 4 skewers

- 4 long woody sprigs of fresh rosemary
- ½ a loaf of rustic white bread, crusts removed
- 12 pitted prunes
- 1¾ ounces soft goat's cheese
- 12 shelled walnut halves
- 6 slices of bacon, the best quality you can afford, halved lengthways
- a small bunch of fresh bay, leaves picked
- olive oil
- sea salt and freshly ground black pepper
- 2 tablespoons quince jelly or apricot jam
- a bunch of fresh thyme
- extra virgin olive oil

The French have such a deep respect for wild food, and these beautiful skewers are my tribute to their wonderful local ingredients. They're quite rustic, and exciting. As you can see, I made these using thick woody rosemary sprigs, the sort you'll see in farmers' markets all over the country or find growing wild. Using rosemary as a skewer is great, because it shares its flavor with the other ingredients. If you can't get woody sprigs, just soak some regular wooden skewers or even cocktail sticks in water and use those instead. If you're having a party, make up a few batches of these and have them standing by ready to cook. They're ridiculously easy to prepare and everyone will love them.

Pick most of the leaves off the rosemary sprigs but leave the ones at the top intact. Cut the bottom of each sprig into a sharp point. Cut the bread into 1½ inch cubes – you'll need 12 in total. Pick up a prune and poke your finger into the hole where the pit used to be, to make the cavity slightly bigger. Spoon and push some soft goat's cheese into the cavity, then press a walnut half into the cheese. Wrap half a slice of bacon around the prune and secure by skewering it on to a rosemary sprig. Thread a bay leaf on next, then a cube of bread and another stuffed prune. Continue doing this until you've used up all your ingredients and have 3 prunes on each skewer. Lay the skewers in a tray.

When you're ready to cook them, preheat your grill pan, grill or even broiler so it's screaming hot. Drizzle olive oil over the tray of skewers, scatter over a good pinch of salt and pepper, and turn each skewer over in the tray until each one is well coated. However you're going to cook them, just make sure you look after them and turn them every minute or so for around 8 to 10 minutes, or until golden, crisp and delightful all over.

Meanwhile, gently heat the quince jelly or apricot jam in a small pan with a splash of water until it's loose enough to paint on to your skewers. Use a pastry brush or a bunch of thyme to lightly paint the warmed jelly all over the skewers. Cook for another minute or so, turning every few seconds so they get sticky and caramelized, then use tongs to move them to a platter. Drizzle over a little extra virgin olive oil and serve straight away.

DUCK CONFIT

Serves 6

- 6 big juicy legs of duck (approximately 10½ ounces each)
- 10 juniper berries
- 4 cloves
- 2 or 3 big handfuls of sea salt
- 6 or 7 fresh bay leaves
- a small bunch of fresh thyme
- 3¾ pounds duck fat

"Confit" means cooked slowly in fat, and it's a method of cooking and preserving born out of necessity in the days before fridges, when people had to make their food last through the cold winter months. Historically people would have had large earthenware containers of this in their larders for months. It might sound complicated, but it's actually really simple, and you're going to love the results. Don't worry about all the fat being used here for cooking and storing, you're not going to eat it - it's there to protect the meat from spoiling and will form a thick layer all over it. You can get duck fat in jars from most specialty food shops. When you cook a piece of duck that's been preserved this way you end up with melt-in-the-mouth meat and skin that's so crisp and wafer thin you'll think you've died and gone to heaven. This recipe is for six duck legs, but you can easily up the quantities to make a larger batch and use the legs as and when you need them. It's perfect for a dinner party, because you can make it weeks in advance if you like.

Put the duck legs into a large roasting pan. Bash the juniper berries and cloves in a pestle and mortar and sprinkle them all over the duck along with the salt. Tear the bay leaves and thyme into the pan, then rub the duck legs really well with the salt and flavorings. Cover the tray with plastic wrap and put it into the fridge or a cold pantry for about 12 hours, or overnight.

The next day, put a large sturdy pan on a low heat. Rinse each of the duck legs under cold water to get rid of the salt, and pat them dry with paper towels.

Put the duck legs into the pan and spoon in all the duck fat. Leave the pan to chug away really slowly on a very low heat for about 2 to 2½ hours, but please keep an eye on the pan and make sure there aren't children running around the kitchen, as hot fat is really dangerous. When the time is up, take the pan off the heat and leave it to cool. If you want to check that the meat is cooked, use tongs to move one of the legs to a plate. Let it cool down, then pinch the meat - you should find it pulls apart really easily.

When everything is nice and cool, ladle some of the fat from the pan into a large earthenware dish or Tupperware container or stainless steel pot and use tongs to put in your duck legs. Carefully pour in the rest of the duck fat, making sure all the meat is completely covered, then cover with plastic wrap or a lid and store in the fridge. It's really important to make sure the meat is completely submerged, as otherwise the fat won't be able to do its job properly and preserve the meat. It will keep perfectly happily in the fridge for weeks if properly covered.

When you want to use the preserved duck legs, pull them out of the hardened fat, wipe any excess away with paper towels, then fry or roast for 15 to 20 minutes, or until the skin is wickedly crisp and the meat is hot through. Or simply tuck in!

DUCK CONFIT ON THE MOST INCREDIBLE LENTILS

Serves 6

- 2 carrots, peeled and finely chopped
- 2 sticks of celery, trimmed and finely chopped
- 2 onions, peeled and finely chopped
- duck fat (or olive oil if you prefer)
- 2½ cups Puy lentils
- 4¼ cups vegetable stock, preferably organic
- 1 potato, peeled and roughly chopped
- 6 legs of duck confit (see previous recipe)
- 7 ounces baby spinach, washed and spun dry
- sea salt and freshly ground black pepper
- extra virgin olive oil
- red wine vinegar
- crème fraîche, to serve

For the bouquet garni
- 1 celery stick
- a small bunch of fresh thyme
- a small bunch of fresh flat-leaf parsley
- 1 fresh bay leaf
- optional: 2 outer leaves of a leek

Lentils aren't really seen as a glamorous thing; in fact they're often considered downright boring. But in this part of France Puy lentils are known as "poor man's caviar" because of their appearance and dark color – and when they're treated really well and seasoned to perfection they're absolutely knockout. Once you've mastered this technique, you'll be able to lean this dish towards any culture: add curry paste to the base for an amazing daal, chuck in some chopped preserved lemons (page 216) and a pinch of cumin seeds for a Moroccan twist, or add a few chopped olives and sun-dried tomatoes, a bit of Swiss chard and some ricotta cheese stirred through at the end for a great Italian vibe. I've made my lentils even more of an event by serving them with incredibly tasty duck confit. The contrast between crispy duck skin, ridiculously soft and tender meat and creamy lentils will blow everyone away.

Preheat your oven to 400°F. Cook the chopped carrots, celery and onions in a large casserole-type pan over medium heat with a tablespoon or two of duck fat (you could also use olive oil here) for around 10 minutes, or until the vegetables have softened but not colored. Make your bouquet garni by wrapping the celery and herbs inside the 2 leek leaves (if using) and tying with string. If you don't have leek leaves, just tie the celery and herbs together. When the veg are in a nice place, add the lentils and give everything a good stir. Pour in your stock, chuck in your potato chunks and add the bouquet garni. Cook for about 45 minutes, stirring occasionally, until your lentils are soft and most of the liquid has been absorbed.

Meanwhile, spoon 6 duck legs out of the confit container and wipe away any excess fat with paper towels. Transfer the legs to a roasting pan and pop it into the top of your hot oven for around 20 to 30 minutes, or until crisp and golden. The meat is already cooked, so what you are trying to achieve here is wafer thin, golden, crispy skin and hot tender meat.

Chop the spinach and stir it into the lentils. Keep cooking for a few more minutes, then take out the bouquet garni. Squash the potato chunks against the side of the pan, then stir them back in. This little trick will lend the lentils some wonderful creaminess. To make these lentils a real joy to eat you now need to think carefully about the flavors. Season to taste with a pinch of salt and pepper, a drizzle of good extra virgin olive oil and 1 or 2 tablespoons of really nice red wine vinegar. Give everything a stir, then check again – it should have a good twang that makes it exciting and will help it cut through the richness of the meat when you serve it.

Remove the duck legs from the pan to a plate lined with paper towels, and pat them dry to soak up the excess fat. Divide the lentils between your serving bowls, then spoon a generous dollop of crème fraîche over each one. Use a knife to gently swirl the crème fraîche into the lentils so you get a wicked marbled effect. Top with a duck leg and serve immediately – to applause from your grateful guests!

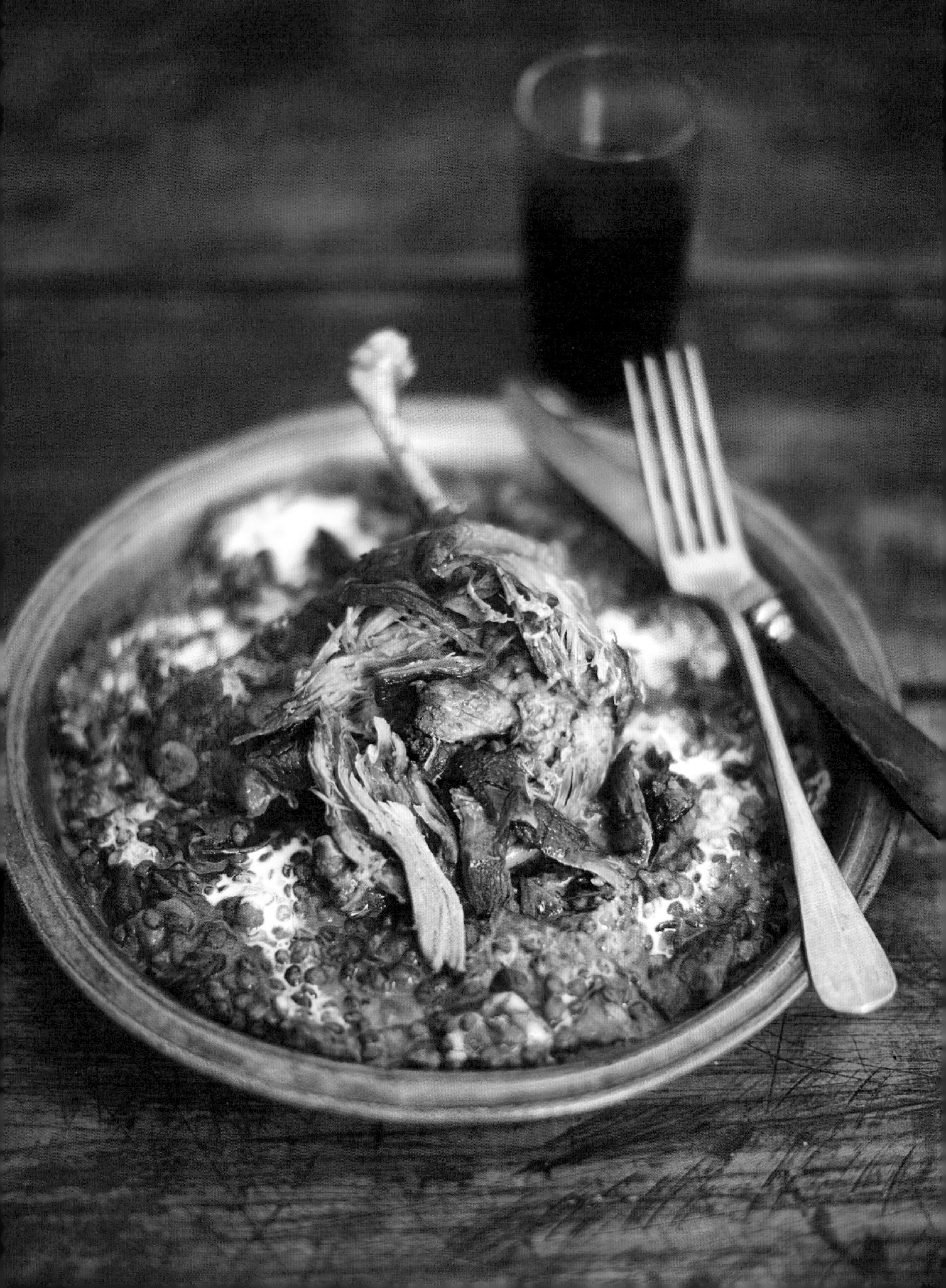

ROMAGES
de
CHEVRES

CRÈME CARAMEL WITH ROASTED PERSIMMONS

Serves 6

For the crème caramel

- 2 cups whole milk
- 1¼ cups granulated sugar
- ½ a vanilla pod, seeds scraped out
- 2 large eggs, preferably free-range or organic
- 2 large egg yolks, preferably free-range or organic

For the roasted persimmons

- 4 large persimmons, or 4 peaches and 6 apricots
- 4 heaped tablespoons raw sugar
- ½ cup Armagnac or brandy

This is a wonderful crème caramel recipe that I learned from a dear friend, Mr. Andy Harris, the editor of my magazine. I've added roasted persimmons because they go beautifully with the silky, delicate texture of the crème caramel. Persimmons are at their absolute best in the autumn. If you've never tried them, they're definitely worth seeking out: taste-wise they have a peachy quality mixed with melon and a hint of lychee, which ain't a bad thing. But feel free to swap in apricots, peaches, strawberries, pears or plums if you're finding them hard to track down. By embracing seasonal fruit, you can serve this dish all year round.

Preheat the oven to 300°F. Heat the milk and ¼ cup of sugar in a medium pan over low heat. Add the vanilla pod and seeds. Once it starts boiling, take the pan off the heat and leave it to stand until completely cool. Get 6 little ramekins or molds out.

To make the caramel, put the remaining sugar into a small non-stick pan with a scant ½ cup of water. Place on a medium heat until the sugar has dissolved, then turn the heat up until the mixture is boiling and bubbling away. Keep it at this heat and after a few minutes the sugar will caramelize and turn a deep golden brown. Make sure you don't touch or taste the caramel, as it can burn badly, and don't be tempted to stir the mixture, just give the pan a gentle swirl every now and then. When it gets to that beautiful caramel color, remove from the heat and quickly and carefully pour into the molds. Leave to set for 5 minutes.

Beat the eggs and yolks together in a bowl, then pour the cooled milk through a fine sieve into the egg mixture. Whisk gently, then pour this mixture through the fine sieve again into a jug. Divide between your ramekins, then put the ramekins in a large roasting pan and create a bain-marie by adding enough hot water to come halfway up the sides. Bake in the middle of the oven for 40 minutes.

Remove the ramekins from the oven and leave to cool, then cover with plastic wrap and pop them into the fridge to set for 4 hours, or overnight. The next day, about 20 minutes before you're ready to serve, preheat your oven to 400°F. Peel and halve the persimmons and cut them into finger-sized segments. If you're using peaches and apricots, halve them and remove the stones. Put the fruit into a small roasting pan, sprinkle over the sugar and drizzle in the Armagnac. Shake the pan so the fruit is nicely coated, and roast in the oven for 20 minutes, or until beautiful and sticky.

Take the pan out of the oven and get your crème caramels out of the fridge. Fill a shallow bowl with hot water and submerge each ramekin three-quarters of the way into the bowl for 30 seconds or so, to loosen the sides. Quickly and confidently turn each caramel out on to a small serving plate and top with a few wedges of roasted fruit. Drizzle any juices from the roasting pan over the top and serve.

THE WORLD-FAMOUS TARTE TATIN

Serves 6

- plain flour, for dusting
- 1 pound puff pastry
- 5 apples (approximately 1½ pounds),
  a mixture of sweet and acidic varieties
- ½ cup raw sugar
- ½ cup Calvados
- 1 vanilla pod, halved lengthways, seeds scraped out
- 3 tablespoons butter, cubed

Not only is this dessert delicious, it was invented quite near where I was staying by the Tatin sisters. The story goes that one of them was making an apple tart but, for whatever reason, made a mistake and left it too long in the oven. However, she thought she could salvage it, so she ended up turning it upside down and her guests went mad for it. I wish all my cooking mistakes had such happy results. If you want to see a video of this being made, go to www.jamieoliver.com/how-to. It's dead simple and when you've made it once you'll have the hang of it.

Hopefully, this recipe will give you the basics so that you'll be able to stretch it by using pears, quinces, peaches, apricots or a mixture ... I'm sure the sisters would love the fact that people were bending this recipe to make it their own. Light golden puff pastry, soft juicy fruit and crisp caramel is a great combination! You could serve this with a spoonful of crème fraîche or whipped cream, but personally I love the contrast between the warm tart and cold ice cream, especially the prune and Armagnac ice cream in the next recipe!

Preheat your oven to 375°F. Dust a clean surface and a rolling pin with flour and roll out your puff pastry until it's just ¼ inch thick. This will be enough to cover the ovenproof frying pan you'll be cooking the tarte Tatin in, leaving about 2 inches extra around the edge. Put the pastry to one side for now. Peel your apples, then halve them horizontally and use a teaspoon to get rid of the seeds and core.

Put the ovenproof pan over medium heat and add the sugar, Calvados, vanilla seeds and pod. Let the sugar dissolve and cook until the mixture forms a light caramel. Just please remember never ever to touch or taste hot caramel, as it can burn really badly.

Once the caramel looks and smells delicious – it should be a lovely chestnut brown – add your halved apples. Carefully stir everything in the pan and cook for about 5 minutes or until the apples start to soften and you get a toffee apple vibe happening. Add the cubed butter, then lay the pastry over the top. Quickly and carefully tuck the pastry down right into the edges – it's best to use a wooden spoon so you don't touch the caramel.

Bake the tarte Tatin for about 25 to 30 minutes, or until golden, with crispy caramelly pieces bubbling up from under the edges. Take it out of the oven. To make it look like a tarte Tatin you need to turn it out, which isn't hard – but you do need to be careful with that hot caramel. So get a serving plate or board larger than your pan and put an oven mitt on to protect the arm holding the board. Put the board or plate on top of the pan, then quickly, carefully and confidently turn it out (remember you can go to www.jamieoliver.com/how-to and see a video of how to do this safely). Put it to one side for a few minutes, so the caramel can cool down, then divide it up and serve with a spoonful of crème fraîche or ice cream.

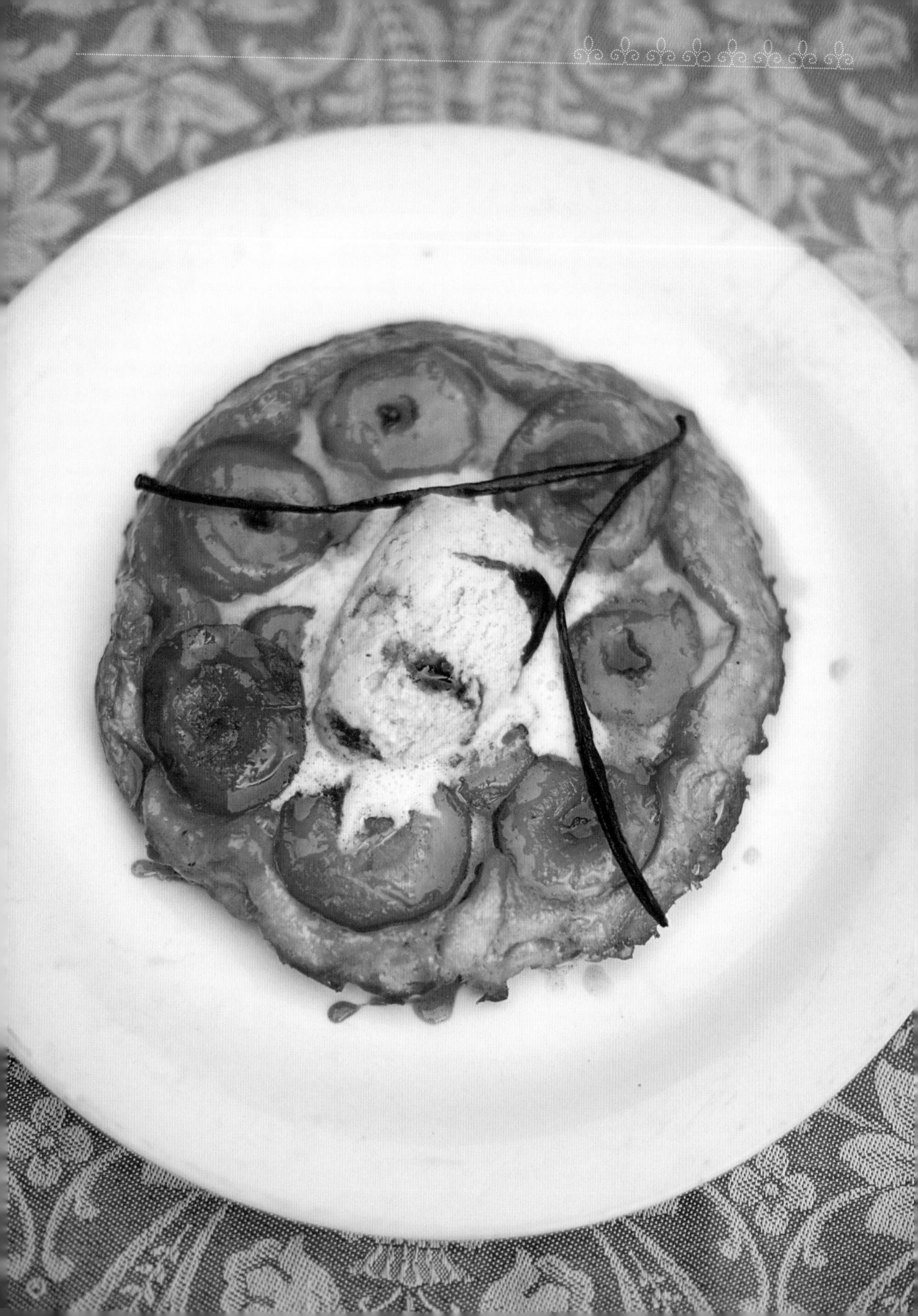

GORGEOUS PRUNE AND ARMAGNAC ICE CREAM

Serves 4-6

For the ice cream

- 1 cup whole milk
- 1 vanilla pod, halved lengthways and seeds scraped out
- 5 large egg yolks, preferably free-range or organic
- 1¼ cups sugar
- 1 cup crème fraîche

For the prune sauce

- 7 ounces prunes, pitted
- 1 cup Armagnac
- ⅓ cup sugar

I've made some delicious ice creams in my day, but this one is particularly special. It uses two ingredients that are a really big deal in the Midi-Pyrénées region where I stayed: prunes and Armagnac, which is a really lovely brandy. Using crème fraîche instead of all cream makes this a slightly less naughty indulgence and also helps to balance out the sweetness of the ice cream and the prune sauce. By blitzing the ice cream after it has set you'll get the smoothest, fluffiest mouthfuls ever, so try this trick at least once. This makes a fairly small batch - enough for about six people to have a good scoop each. If you're an ice cream lover, just double the amount here.

Gently heat the milk with the vanilla pod and seeds in a pan over medium heat. Just before it starts to boil, take it off the heat and fish out the vanilla pod. In a little bowl, whisk the egg yolks and sugar together until creamy then immediately whisk that into the hot milk mixture followed by the crème fraîche. Put aside and leave to cool. Once cool, pour into a suitable dish, cover with plastic wrap and pop into the freezer for at least 4 hours, or until completely frozen.

While your ice cream is freezing, get started on the prune sauce. Pop your prunes and Armagnac into a small pan and leave to soak for 30 minutes. Add the sugar to the pan and gently bring everything to the boil. Turn the heat down and simmer for 5 minutes, until thick and syrupy. Blitz with an immersion blender so you have a glossy, smooth and jammy mixture - dilute with more Armagnac or a splash of water to loosen if needed. Leave to cool, then cover and put into the fridge so it's chilled by the time your ice cream comes out of the freezer.

Once the ice cream has set, take the dish out of the freezer and let it sit for about 5 minutes. Spoon the ice cream into a food processor. Give it a good blitz so it's nice and creamy (but work quickly so it doesn't melt), then return it to the dish and cover with plastic wrap. Put back into the freezer for about an hour.

When the hour is up, check on your ice cream. It should be frozen but soft now, so take it out of the freezer and pour that cold prune mixture on top. Spoon and fold it through the ice cream a handful of times so you get a beautiful marble effect. Reserve any extra sauce to serve with your next batch of ice cream. Cover the finished ice cream with plastic wrap and return it to the freezer so it is ready whenever you want it.

WALNUT, CHESTNUT AND CHOCOLATE CAKE

Serves 10

- a knob of butter, for greasing
- 1 cup shelled walnuts
- 3½ ounces peeled, cooked chestnuts
- 1¾ ounces good-quality dark chocolate (70% cocoa solids)
- 2 cups self-rising flour
- zest of 1 orange
- 1 cup raw sugar, plus an extra teaspoon
- 4 large eggs, preferably free-range or organic
- 1¼ cups heavy cream
- ¼ cup whole milk
- 1 vanilla pod, halved lengthways, seeds scraped out
- 10 ounce can sweetened chestnut purée
- 1 tablespoon roasted coffee beans

In any rural area where there's a glut of a particular ingredient - walnuts in the Midi-Pyrénées, for example - you'll see them pop up in all sorts of recipes. Like this cake, which makes the most incredible tea-time indulgence. The locals love the combination of coffee and walnuts, so I've dusted a hint of coffee over the beautiful chestnut purée and whipped cream filling. Sweetened chestnut purée is a really popular French ingredient, and can be found at specialty food shops. You can also buy regular chestnut purée and sweeten it yourself (see my P.S. at the end of this recipe). Cutting the cake in half this way is dead easy, but if you need a little more guidance go to www.jamieoliver.com/how-to and watch a video of it being done.

Preheat your oven to 350°F. Grease a 9-inch round springform cake tin with a knob of butter, then line the base with parchment paper.

Tip the walnuts, chestnuts and chocolate into a food processor and pulse for around 10 seconds, or until you have a mixture of smooth and small choppy pieces. Sift in your flour, and add the zest of 1 orange and the sugar. Crack in the eggs and pour in ½ cup of heavy cream, and the milk. Blitz until just combined – no more.

Spoon your mixture into your prepared pan and bake your cake in the hot oven for around 35 to 40 minutes. Check on it after 35 minutes, and insert a small knife or cocktail stick into the center of the cake. If it comes out clean, it's done (there may be a little melted chocolate on the skewer, but as long as there's no raw cake batter you're good to go). Remove from the oven and leave to cool in the pan for 10 minutes, then carefully take out of the pan and leave on a wire rack to cool completely.

When the cake has cooled, whip the rest of your cream in a bowl with a teaspoon of sugar and the vanilla seeds until it forms soft peaks, then put aside. Get yourself a long knife and run it around the middle of the cake, scoring and turning as you go, until the two lines join up (remember you can go to www.jamieoliver.com/how-to to see a video of how this is done). Carefully start turning and cutting into your cake, going deeper each time until you end up with two round halves, like you see in the picture. Spoon and spread the chestnut purée over the base of the cake and top with the whipped cream. Pound your coffee beans in a pestle and mortar until you get a powder, then use a fine sieve to sprinkle them all over the cream. Pop the top back on the cake and treat all your friends to a slice.

P.S. To make your own sweet chestnut purée, put a scant ¾ cup into a pan with ½ cup of **milk**. Bring it to the boil, then simmer for 2 to 3 minutes. Remove from the heat and mash in half a 15-ounce can of **chestnut purée**. Blitz with an immersion blender until fairly smooth, and pop into the fridge until you need it.

THE SWEETEST PUMPKIN TART

Serves 12

For the pastry

- 1¼ cups flour, plus extra for dusting
- ¼ cup confectioners' sugar
- ½ cup good-quality unsalted cold butter, cut into small cubes
- 1 large egg, preferably free-range or organic, beaten
- a splash of milk
- olive oil, for greasing the tart tin

For the filling

- 1 x 1-pound cheese or sugar pumpkin, peeled, deseeded and diced into 1 inch chunks
- 2 cups whole milk
- 1 cup raw sugar
- 1 vanilla pod, halved lengthways and seeds scraped out
- 2 large eggs, preferably free-range or organic

I stumbled across this beautiful dessert, or at least one element of it, at a fantastic little restaurant called Lou Bourdie in a village called Bach. Monique, the lovely owner, had baked a panful of a delicious pumpkin dessert, and was serving small squares of it to her customers. The sweet pumpkin mixture had cooked and set like a sort of rustic crème caramel, and it was so delicious I had to make my own version. I've put mine into a pastry tart, because that contrast between short crumbly pastry and soft silky filling is magic. Enjoy!

You can make your pastry by hand, or in a food processor. From a height, sieve your flour and confectioners' sugar into a large mixing bowl. Using your fingertips, gently work the butter into the flour and sugar until the mixture resembles breadcrumbs. Add the egg and milk and gently work it together using your hands until you have a ball. Don't work the pastry too much or it will become elastic and chewy, not crumbly and short.

Sprinkle some flour over the dough and a clean work surface, and pat the ball into a thick flat round. Sprinkle over a little more flour, then wrap the pastry in plastic wrap and pop it into the fridge to rest for 30 minutes. Lightly oil the inside of a 10-inch non-stick loose-bottomed tart pan. Dust a clean surface and a rolling pin with flour, and carefully roll out your pastry, turning and dusting it every so often, until you've got a circle about ¼ inch thick. Roll the pastry over the rolling pin, then unroll it into the pan, making sure you push it into the sides. Trim off any extra and use that to patch any holes, then prick the base of the case all over with a fork, cover with plastic wrap, and pop it into the freezer for 30 minutes. Preheat your oven to 350°F.

Meanwhile, put the pumpkin, milk, sugar, vanilla pod and its seeds into a small deep pan on a medium heat. Keep stirring so nothing catches, and turn the heat down to low just as it comes to the boil. Simmer for about 15 minutes, stirring occasionally, then put a lid half on and cook for a further 15 minutes, or until the pumpkin is tender and cooked through. Remove from the heat, discard the vanilla pod, and use an immersion blender to carefully blitz until silky and smooth. Put aside to cool and pop the lid on the pan to stop a skin forming.

While your pumpkin mixture cools, lay a large piece of parchment paper over your pastry, pushing it right into the sides. Fill the paper right up to the top with uncooked rice, and bake for 10 minutes in your hot oven. Take the case out, carefully remove the rice (saving it for another time) and parchment paper, and return the pastry to the oven to cook for a further 10 minutes, until it's firm and almost cookie-like. Leave to cool completely, and turn the oven down to 325°F.

Beat the 2 eggs together, add them to the pumpkin mixture and blitz again. Pour this mixture into your pastry base, then bake in the hot oven for around 30 minutes, or until the mixture has set but still has a slight wobble to it. Leave to cool, then serve with a drizzle of cream or a spoonful of crème fraîche and dive in.

pecialites
du pays

WINE, ARTISAN BREAD, CHEESES, BOUQUET GARNI, MUSTARD AND GARLIC

Wine plays a huge role in French culture, not only as a drink, but also as a flavoring in cooking. The daily buying of **bread**, whether a humble baguette or artisan loaf, is almost a religion in France. Every region has its own distinct and wonderful **cheeses** such as Normandy's camembert, or Burgundy's Epoisses. Fresh and dried herbs are often tied together in a **bouquet garni** and cooked in soups and stews for added flavor. French **mustards** can be hot and strong or mild and sweet. **Garlic** grown in the Pyrénées is considered some of the best in the world.

VINEGARS, DUCK OR GOOSE FAT, WALNUTS, PRUNES, PUY LENTILS AND CHARCUTERIE

French **vinegars** are aged in barrels to develop their lovely sharp flavor. **Duck or goose fat** is often used as a preservative (for confit) and also for cooking in place of oil or butter. **Walnuts** grow in the forests of the Midi-Pyrénées and show up in many cakes and biscuits. **Prunes** from Agen, near Cahors, are considered the country's best. They are often poached in brandy, then used in cakes or tarts. **Puy lentils** form the base of countless classic French peasant dishes. Duck, goose, pork, venison and wild boar are just a few of the meats that are smoked, cured or dried in the process known as **charcuterie**.

"Lord" Loftus

The one & only Mike

My dear Ginny

HACEMOS
CARNES Y
PESCADOS
A LA
BARBACOA
EN
NUESTRA
TERRAZA

Andy "in translation" Harris

Gorgeous Georgie

Large Louis

Greek Mihalis & Saffa S

Lovely Laura

Main-man Luke

Perfect Dave

The Great "Goaders"

Pete "the meat"

"Scouser" Nic

Sarah "Tiddles"

Lou "M"

Darling pregnant Lana

Thank You ...

So many people worked incredibly hard to help me make this book. You all did a wonderful job and I thank you from the bottom of my heart for making it such a pleasure to work on ... If I've left anyone off the list by mistake, give me a shout and I'll get you into the reprint!

As always, my love and thanks to the lovely Jools and our three gorgeous girls, Poppy, Daisy and Petal. You put up with me being away and always make coming home such a joy. Love to Mum and Dad for their support, and to my surrogate relative, the always inspiring Italian Stallion Gennaro Contaldo. I've said it before but I'll say it again. I've got the best damn food team in the entire world! To Ginny Rolfe, Sarah Tildesley, Georgie Socratous, Anna Jones, Pete Begg, Claire Postans, Bobby Sebire, Christina McCloskey, Laura Parr, Daniel Nowland, Joanne Lord and Helen Martin: you are a joy to work with and I love you all dearly. To Siobhan Boyle for her hard work in Spain, as well as for all her work testing. And to Abigail "Scottish" Fawcett, Laura Fyfe and Kate McCullough for their further work testing, many thanks. **To David Loftus: mate, although you have terminal IBS it doesn't stop you taking the most fantastic photos! Here's to our tenth beautiful book together.** To the cracking editorial team who pulled this book off in record time: the mad but creative genius that is Andy Harris, and his sidekick on this project, my lovely editor Katie Bosher. Thanks for everything, you two. Big thanks as well to my word girls Rebecca "Rubs" Walker and Bethan O'Connor. **Massive shout out to Interstate Associates** – the brilliant designers who took my words and David's pictures and turned them into this beautiful book. I'm hugely grateful to all of you for pouring as much hard work and love into this project as we have. The results speak for themselves! To the lovely Jayne Connell, and to two of my favourite Essex girls, Louise Caton and Lucy Self (see you at Duke's some time!); to Brian Simpson, for introducing me to a whole new way of working, and to James Jeanes and Ben Watts. And, of course, to the wonderful gang at Penguin who always get behind whatever I do and make sure we end up with something fantastic: big love and thanks to Tom Weldon and Louise Moore for their support, and to my good mates art director John Hamilton and cookery publisher Lindsey Evans; and well done to the ever-efficient Juliette Butler, and to Keith Taylor, Nick Lowndes and Laura Herring for keeping us on track. Thanks also to Clare Pollock, Chantal Noel, Kate Brotherhood, Elizabeth Smith, Jen Doyle, Anna Rafferty, Naomi Fidler and Thomas Chicken. Biggest love as well to the fantastic Annie Lee, Helen Campbell, Caroline Pretty and Caroline Wilding for all their hard work. We couldn't have made such a beautiful book without Fresh One getting us to these incredible and beautiful places. To Zoe Collins, Jo Ralling, Roy Ackerman, Nicola Gooch, Emma Palmer-Watts, Sophie Alcock, Alex Buxton, Jonathan Knapp, Chloe Huntly and Gudsen Claire. And to my core TV crew on these trips (many of whom are in these snapshots here) – you worked bloody hard and were up for every experience, as per usual: my dear Lana Salah (if you have a boy you'd better call him Jamie!), Nicolanne "Scouser" Cox, Laura Abrahams, Sally Wingate, Katie Millard, Luke "Coconut Balls" Cardiff, Mike Sarah, Godfrey Kirby, Louise Caulfield, Dave Miller (such perfect hair!), Simon Weekes, Pete Bateson, Mihalis Margaritis, Craig Loveridge, Olly Wiggins, and Jeff Brown. On each of these trips we had the most brilliant support from local tourist boards, caterers and translators. Thanks so much for all you did for us. To the fantastic fixers we had – you and your teams worked hard and did an amazing job. In Spain, Richard Webb and his crew, René Zuber in Stockholm, Tim Buxton and his guys in Marrakesh, Nicola Rosada in Venice, Nico Mangriotis in Greece and Victoria Clement and Fabienne Boussier in France. It takes a lot of careful planning and work to make things run smoothly behind the scenes, so I want to give big verbal hugs to my amazing personal team. My dear friend and ally Louise "M" Holland, Liz McMullan, Holly Adams, Saffron Greening, Beth Richardson and Paul Rutherford. I really couldn't do it without you, so thanks for taking such good care of me. And to the guys at my offices who do incredible work for me day in and day out – thanks and love: to my CEO, John Jackson, MD Tara Donovan and their teams, from online to marketing, PR and accounts... the list goes on – love and thanks to you all! Last, but certainly not least, a huge thanks to all the beautiful people I met on my travels, many of whom appear in this book. There isn't nearly enough room to name all of you, but without fail, I was met by smiles and warmth wherever I went and I came back inspired, excited and with fantastic memories.

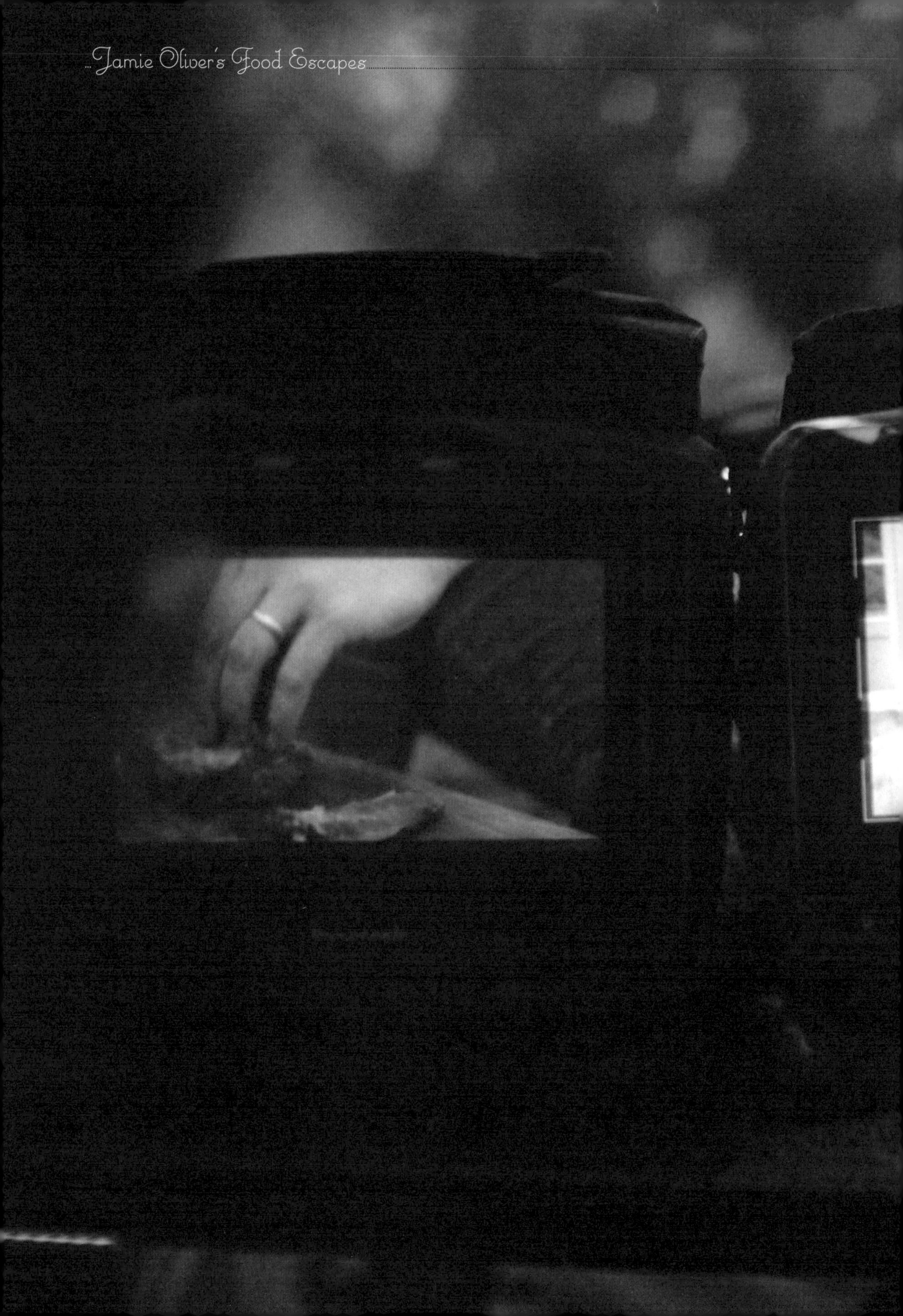

Index

- Page references in **bold** indicate an illustration
- Entries in *blue* indicate an essential ingredient described in one of the six chapters
- v indicates a vegetarian recipe